Chase the Game

Also by Pat Jordan

Black Coach
The Suitors of Spring
A False Spring
Broken Patterns

Chase the Game

Pat Jordan

Dodd, Mead & Company ● New York

Copyright © 1979 by Pat Jordan
All rights reserved
No part of this book may be reproduced in any form
without permission in writing from the publisher
Printed in the United States of America

1 2 3 4 5 6 7 8 9 10

Library of Congress Cataloging in Publication Data

Jordan, Pat.
   Chase the game.

   1. Oleynick, Frank. 2. McLeod, Barry.
3. Luckett, Walter. 4. Basketball players—United
States—Biography. I. Title.
GV884.A1J67   796.32′3′0922 [B]   78-31848
ISBN 0-396-07632-7

For Frank, Barry and Walter

prologue

Frank Oleynick, Barry McLeod and Walter Luckett are lifelong friends who grew up together in and around the various black ghettos of Bridgeport, Connecticut, during the late 1960s and early 1970s. Oleynick and McLeod, first cousins, are white. Luckett is black. Their backgrounds, however—their families, friends and life-styles—are, at times, so similar as to seem interchangeable. Like most ghetto youths, all three turned early to sports for their satisfactions. Eventually sports became an outlet for their frustrations and, ultimately, a means of escape from their surroundings. Their personalities have been defined in large measure by their participation in sports, and most of the influences over their lives can be traced to that participation.

As youngsters, they played baseball, basketball and football—and were successful at each. Then, in their early teens, they turned exclusively to basketball. They excelled in this sport to varying degrees, first in high school and then at college, where each received a basketball scholarship. All three fulfilled a longstanding dream when drafted by a team in the National Basketball Association. None of this, however, makes their lives any more noteworthy than those of thousands of youths with similar backgrounds. The lives of these three are recorded here not because of their similarity to the lives of others, but because of those details that make their stories unique. And they are. Oleynick and McLeod are white, and Luckett is black, and although the turn of their lives was certainly affected by their race, this did not happen in a way one would expect. Their lives were also affected by their common friends and life-styles and success in sports, and by their identical family backgrounds. But again, such common threads did not weave similar tapestries.

Now, in their mid-twenties, their lives still touch. Their families, friends and life-styles are the same. And they are still close, although not as close as they once were. They are too different for that now, and they are far too different from the days when as youngsters they played together on city streets. Their devotion to basketball has changed too, although in individual ways. The only thing that hasn't changed is that their lives were, still are, and always will be profoundly influenced by a simple game invented by a bookish-looking college professor to alleviate his gym students' boredom during the long, cold New England winter of 1891.

one

Dr. James Naismith was born on a farm in Almonte, Ontario, Canada, on November 6, 1861. Orphaned at eight, he was raised by a bachelor uncle. He attended McGill University and the Presbyterian Theological Seminary in Montreal, hoping someday to become a minister. In his late twenties, however, he decided there were other effective ways of doing good besides preaching, and so he turned to sports. He enrolled at the International YMCA Training School, soon to become Springfield College, in Springfield, Massachusetts, and eventually became a professor there. He taught a gymnasium class. As was the custom then, he made his students do calisthenics and tumble and march and play leapfrog. His students grew bored and complained to the dean. Dr. Naismith admitted his class was boring and his students were losing interest. "What this new generation wanted," he said, "was pleasure and thrill, as in football, rather than physical benefits only."

He thought about this problem for two weeks. Then, in November 1891, Dr. Naismith nailed an empty peach basket against the overhead track that circled the gymnasium ten feet above the floor. He divided his class of nineteen students into two teams, handed them a soccer ball and read them thirteen rules. The most significant rule was number eight: "A goal shall be made when the ball is thrown or batted from the grounds into the basket and stays there, providing those defending the goal do not touch or disturb the goal. If the ball rests on the edge and the opponent moves the basket, it shall count as a goal." The nineteenth student stood on a stepladder underneath the basket and, when a goal was scored, reached into the basket and returned the ball to the players.

Dr. Naismith's game became one of the world's most popular sports. Yet when he died on November 28, 1939, he still did not grasp the extent of that popularity. Once, in 1937, he saw 18,000 people at a game in Madison Square Garden. "Good heavens," he said, "all these people would come to watch basketball?" He never clapped or yelled at a game. He sat almost perfectly still and silent, leaning slightly forward in his seat, not with anticipation but with a look of wonder on his owlish face. He wore wire-rimmed oval spectacles, sported a brushlike mustache and favored tweed suits. He was too short and stocky to play successfully the game he invented. In his later years, finally, he did resemble a minister. He said he had invented his game simply to help mankind enjoy leisure time. He would never comprehend the profound impact basketball would have on the lives of the people who would play it.

If Dr. Naismith never grasped the significance of basketball, others did. On February 18, 1968, in Springfield, Massachusetts, the Naismith Memorial Basketball Hall of Fame was completed, as modest in size and scope as its progenitor. It stands on the edge of the Springfield College campus amid failing Victorian homes at the end of a tiny road called Hall of Fame Street. The Memorial is a rectangular, red brick building with only a plaque to differentiate it from the thousands of grammar schools it resembles. Inside are three floors of basketball memorabilia.

The most interesting exhibits are on the Memorial's main floor, where there is an Honors Court for every contributor, coach and player elected to the Hall of Fame. It is a dark and reverential room with walls entirely of stained glass windows—made actually of plastic—in which are embedded a portrait and brief biography of each member. Dr. Naismith is here. "Phog" Allen is here. "Hank" Luisetti is here. George Mikan is here. Christian Steinmetz is here. Clair Bee is here. John Wooden is here. Amos Alonzo Stagg is here. Harlan Page is here. "Ned" Irish is here. Nat Holman is here. Joe Lapchick is here. Adolph Rupp is here. "Dutch" Dehnert is here. "Red" Auerbach is here. Bob Cousy is here, and so is Bill Russell, the first black player elected individually to the Hall of Fame.

A section of the Honors Court is reserved for the four teams in the almost ninety-year history of the game that have been enshrined, as a team, in the Hall. The first team so honored was Dr. Naismith's original gymnasium class of 1891. The players are stern-looking men with mustaches like the Sundance Kid's. The second team elected was the Buffalo Germans, organized in 1895 by Frederick Burkhardt, a wild-eyed man also with a mustache. The Germans were thought to be the best basketball team in the world from 1904 to 1910. They won at the Pan American Exposition in Buffalo in 1901, when they played in cleats on a 40′ by 60′ court. The Buffalo players, such as the two Alfreds, Heerdt and

Manweiller, were clean-shaven and more youthful-looking than Dr. Naismith's Springfield players. They were, in fact, frail-looking, sleepy-eyed young men who slicked down their hair and parted it in the middle.

The third team elected to the Hall also had a northern European name, the Original Celtics. The Celts were the first great professional team, winning the American Professional League championship in 1926–27 and 1927–28. Its stars were Joe Lapchick, "Dutch" Dehnert, Nat Holman, "Horse" Haggerty and Ernie Reich. To a man they had the classic, sharply chiseled features of their supposed Celtic origins.

The last team elected to the Hall was the New York Renaissance or the New York Rens or, as they were often called, the Harlem Rens. The Rens were considered the finest team in the world from 1932 to 1936; they won 473 games and lost 49, and during the 1933–34 season fashioned an eighty-eight-game winning streak. Their stars were Eyre Saitch, Clarence "Fat" Jenkins, Bill Yancey, James "Pappy" Ricks, "Tarzan" Cooper and "Wee Willie" Smith. Saitch was an inordinately handsome man who could have passed for Clark Gable's brother except that his skin was black like the rest of his teammates—the first of their race to master the game they now dominate.

Also on the main floor of the Memorial is an exact replica of the gymnasium in which Dr. Naismith first nailed up his peach basket. It is complete with stepladder, overhead track and the original peach basket. The rest of the room contains exhibits tracing the growth of his invention. There is the first soccer ball used by Dr. Naismith, the long gray uniform pants worn by his gymnasium class, the first quilted and padded shorts worn by a basketball team and the coarse woolen uniforms worn by the Original Celtics. There are more recent exhibits, too, such as the uniform worn by Bevo Francis of Rio Grande College when he scored 113 points in a collegiate game; the uniform worn by Wilt Chamberlain when he scored 100 points in an NBA game; the basketball used to record the longest successful shot in a game (84' 11") and another in which a college player recorded his sixty-fifth consecutive successful free throw. Bob Lanier's sneakers are there, too, for they are the largest ever worn by a player: size 20.

The criteria for which such memorabilia are enshrined are simple, says Lee Williams, the Memorial's executive director. "The events commemorated must reflect a significant moment in the history of the game. The first, the last, the most, the least, the highest, the lowest, the longest—things like that. We do not try, however, to make judgments on 'the greatest.' We let others determine such things and we just reflect their judgments. For example, we have recently opened a High School Room in the basement. It would be beyond us to determine who was the greatest high school player in the country each year, so we leave that to other 'experts' like, say, *Sports Illustrated* magazine. We would just record their judgment for history."

The High School Room contains the basketball used by Ashland, Kentucky, when it defeated Canton, Illinois, 15–10 for the First National High School Championship in 1928. It has photographs of the various Passaic, New Jersey, High School "wonder teams" that won 159 consecutive games from 1919 to 1925. On dummy torsos roped off from other exhibits are the uniforms of several high school players whose achievements were deemed significant enough to warrant being immortalized. There is the uniform of Tom McMillen, now with the New York Knicks, who was the first high school player to have his photograph on the cover of *Sports Illustrated*. There is the uniform of Moses Malone, now with the Houston Rockets, who was the first high school player drafted directly into professional basketball. And there is the uniform of Walter Luckett, Jr., the No. 1 draft choice of the Detroit Pistons in 1975, who was generally thought to be the greatest high school basketball player in the world in 1972.

During his four-year high school career in Bridgeport, Connecticut, Luckett scored more points—2691—than any player in New England history. He averaged 31½ points per game over that span, and his 39½ per game average in his senior year was the second highest mark in the country. He converted over 60 percent of his field goal attempts. Today Pete Maravich, the greatest offensive player in the National Basketball Association, converts less than 45 percent of his shots. Like Maravich, Luckett was a guard. He stood only 6'3" and made many shots from distances greater than 25 feet from the basket. Most of the 200 or so college scouts who followed him call him the greatest pure shooter the game has ever seen.

Luckett's shooting skill was a complement to his other talents. When an opposing team used a full-court press, Luckett's teammates would pass him the ball under their own basket and would then vacate that half of the court while he dribbled through the opposition. When he crossed half-court he either shot immediately from distances as great as 35 feet or hit one of his teammates (often in the head) with a pass they neither saw nor expected. In his senior year Luckett averaged thirteen assists per game. If there was a missed shot, more often than not Luckett grabbed the rebound; he averaged sixteen rebounds per game as a senior. He also checked the opposition's best scorer. From the stands he appeared to be a shade slow for a guard, but on the court he moved with such grace and economy of effort that he was often compared to Walt Frazier and Oscar Robertson. Like those two great players, he maneuvered deliberately, as if calculating each move before executing it. He played less on instinct than on intelligence. On offense, Luckett never turned his back on his man to spin left-right-left-right à la Earl Monroe. Holding the ball low between his legs, Luckett faced his man squarely, looked him in the eye to read him, then made his move. His fakes and feints were subtle and often imperceptible to the fans in the stands who never saw the flick of his eyes or the quick shift of his shoulders, and so wondered how he always managed to get off his shots without being contested. He never humiliated his defender, never left him grasping at air. He left him paralyzed, flat-footed, looking up pitifully as Luckett lofted yet another successful jump shot. Luckett's genius lay in his ability to know without seeing when his defender's weight had shifted left, or right, or when he was unprepared, and he had the split-second timing that enabled him to take advantage of this.

Luckett was not a temperamental player. His game was cool and self-assured without being arrogant. He was unselfish to a fault. Once when his high school team lost an important game to their arch rival, Walter was held responsible for that loss because he had not taken enough shots. In fact, he had taken twenty-four shots and converted twenty of them, scoring forty-eight points in all—which, at that time, was only four points above his season's average.

Luckett had so mastered Dr. Naismith's game in 1972 that there was talk he might go directly into the pros from high school, the first player and the only backcourt man ever to do this. Rumor had it that he would play in the American Basketball Association for two years and then, after his game had matured a bit, would leap into the NBA. The rumor never came true, for Luckett chose to accept a scholarship from Ohio University in Athens, Ohio. It was only one of the 200 or so offers he had received from every major college in the country, including UCLA, Maryland, Notre Dame and Providence, all of which had sent so many scouts to his every high school contest that they often outnumbered the fans.

Before Luckett played his first game at Ohio University, his picture appeared on the cover of the November 27, 1972, issue of *Sports Illustrated,* featuring a story that claimed he was the best freshman college basketball player in the country. Luckett's high school career had given the magazine's editors ample evidence on which to base this opinion, but that was not the only criterion for deciding to use his picture on the cover. It seems that in 1972 Walter Luckett was blessed not only with talent but also with luck. For years the black community had accused *Sports Illustrated* of being a racist publication because it used too few cover shots of black athletes in proportion to those of whites. The magazine editors claimed that when pictures of blacks were used, recognizability suffered on newsstands and the magazine appeared dark and infinitely less visible than other more colorful publications. The editors further admitted that they actually sought out light-skinned black athletes whose skin tones would reproduce satisfactorily enough to be used for a cover. That was why those editors were only too eager to put this freshman's picture on their November 27, 1972, issue. Walter Luckett was black, or rather he was *a* black, since actually his skin was the color of the hardwood floors on which he played.

That cover shows Luckett wearing a white Ohio U. uniform trimmed in green. He is hunched forward, his arms and legs spread, about to bounce a basketball into the open jaws of a bobcat (the Ohio mascot), whose angry visage is painted at midcourt of the school's Convocation Center. Luckett's skin melts into the caramel-colored court. He is long-limbed, lean and faintly muscled. His lightly tensed pose exudes a look of feline grace, which is marred only by the lumpy white brace on his left knee, injured at the close of his senior year in high school. Over the summer of 1972 he underwent knee surgery and at the time the cover was being shot, his knee had not yet healed. Fluid was constantly being drained from it and the pain was excruciating, but it does not show on his face. It is a handsome face, long and narrow and topped by a modest Afro. He has a straight nose and pouty, slightly parted lips. He is looking up at the camera as if at his man, the defender. He is trying to read him. His eyes are deep brown. They look puzzled.

two

When Walter Luckett was in eighth grade he scored fifty-nine points against a high school junior varsity team. When he was a sophomore in high school he scored fifty-three points against a varsity team. When he was a junior in college he scored twenty-eight points against a team of professionals led by Julius Erving and John Williamson. His career, particularly in high school, was a succession of such games, each so nearly approaching perfection that people who regularly saw him play grew to expect of him mere brilliance. And Luckett never let them become jaded. Whenever his talent seemed to have reached its zenith—forty-six points, thirty-one rebounds, fifteen assists—he would reply with an even greater effort—fifty-one points, thirty rebounds, seven assists—which, anew, left his fans breathless. He was like a demented rock musician determined to exceed his fans' wildest expectations with increasingly outrageous performances. Ultimately, it seemed, his final encore would be to self-destruct.

People who never saw him play assumed the games blurred one into another until no one game could be distinguished, leaving nothing but an empty stage and a smoke-shrouded mass of points, rebounds and assists.

But that was not the case. One game stands out above all the rest. It came near the end of his senior year in high school, shortly before he injured his knee. It was the kind of game that could sustain an athlete in reveries long after his career had ended. It was also the kind where the number of fans who claimed to have seen it grew each year until today almost 10,000 people say they witnessed an event played in a gymnasium that seated 800. For many of the spectators it would be the greatest basketball game they would ever see. Yet it was meaningless, with no city or state championship at stake; both teams played in different state and city divisions.

It was not without meaning for the players involved, however, since they had grown up together in the city's ghettos. They had played with or against each other for all of their basketball playing lives. As they grew older, their allegiances shifted from the neighborhood to the boys' clubs and then to the grammar schools. This constant shifting prevented any serious rivalries from developing since a player who might have been a teammate on a boys' club state team a year ago could be an opponent at a different grammar school a year later. Rivalries solidified only when the best players gravitated to one of the city's two parochial high schools. There, cleanly divided into two camps, they grew in intensity until, by the players' senior year, they were as fierce as only such things can be among ghetto youths for whom the rules and structure of basketball are often the only order in their lives. And so this game between the two best teams in the city—and possibly the state—had a significance for its players that went beyond anything most people could comprehend. It would give the winners not a city title or a state crown but bragging rights as the best team in the city at every ghetto court and drugstore and gymnasium where the players on both teams were constantly meeting.

Walter Luckett played for Kolbe, an all-male high school in the heart of the city's slums. It was run by an order of Franciscan friars. They wore sandals, coarse brown cassocks and ropes around their stomachs, most of which were ample. Their founder had been famous for feeding birds, and his followers had a similar reputation. Unlike the Jesuits, who were known for fierce intellectual disciplines, the friars had a kind of rustic amiability that seemed more suited to Sherwood Forest than to a tough inner-city school outside the doors of which drug addicts and prostitutes roamed. That amiability, however, was infinitely more valuable than any intellectual pursuits could be for Kolbe's 200 or so black, Puerto Rican and poor ethnic whites, few of whom would ever go to college. The friars had no intellectual pretensions. They merely hoped to break down the ghetto rage and cynicism on which their students had been raised and to which they returned each afternoon.

Kolbe's basketball rival, Notre Dame, was also an all-male city high school, located far north of the inner city near the suburbs of Fairfield and Trumbull. Notre Dame was surrounded by grass and trees and a public golf course. It had a baseball diamond and a football field. It had a parking lot, and some of its students drove to school. Kolbe had no parking lot, nor did its students need one since most of them lived within walking distance of the school and all were too poor to own a car. Kolbe's few lay teachers who drove to school had to park their cars on the street. Whenever possible they sneaked a glance out of their classroom windows to make sure their cars were still there.

Notre Dame's students were taught by the Holy Cross fathers. They were generally younger and leaner than the friars and, in the late 1960s, tended to wear Army fatigues and black turtleneck sweaters. Only a handful of their students were black or Puerto Rican; the majority were lower-middle-class ethnic whites—Poles, Slovaks, Irish, Italians—whose parents were only one short economic step removed from their Kolbe counterparts. Ironically, the black, the Puerto Rican and the white ethnic parents had started out life in Bridgeport on the same rung of the city's economic ladder. They had once lived side by side and many of them still did—the blacks and Puerto Ricans in ghetto housing projects and the ethnic whites across the street in ramshackle homes. They shared an uneasy truce, unlike their children who mingled freely, and became friends. Those friendships were formed on the city's streets, were nurtured in Little League, the boys' clubs and grammar school, and were disrupted when it came time to go to high school. By then, the whites had made their short economic leap over their black and Puerto Rican neighbors who, for various and obvious reasons, were as economically depressed as before. Both groups, however, felt an obligation to send their children to one of the city's parochial high schools, which had identical tuitions of $600.

The Catholic Church and other state and civic organizations helped subsidize that tuition for the blacks and Puerto Ricans, but only rarely did so for the whites, and then only for the poorest of them. Since the whites felt no hardship was too great to get their children out of the ghetto, they added to their expense by choosing to send their children far across town to Notre Dame. This necessitated either buying them an inexpensive car, giving them money each day for the bus or waking early to drive them to school before they went off to work in one of the city's factories. Their black and Puerto Rican neighbors could afford none of these alternatives, in many cases had no car of their own, and so it was inevitable that their children would walk through the city's streets to Kolbe.

Once in high school, the two groups of friends began to form new friendships more along the social lines they would find comfortable in later years. When they returned in the afternoon to their homes they confronted one another now as rivals, albeit still friendly ones, and taunted each other as to which of their schools had the best basketball team in the city. At the time Kolbe had a 10–2 record while Notre Dame was 13–0.

Kolbe was coached by Lennie Lee, a slim, handsome, easygoing man in his twenties who had once been a modestly successful guard at Notre Dame High School and later at Panhandle A & M College in Panhandle, Texas. He was one of the first white basketball players in Bridgeport to be able to dribble a basketball between his legs. He had picked up that flamboyant move at one of Bob Cousy's summer basketball camps, but had not stayed long enough to pick up some of Cousy's discipline too. His teams played a ghetto game not unlike that played today by the University of Nevada-Las Vegas. They always opted for the flashy play. Their defense was their offense. On defense they overplayed their man in anticipation of a stolen pass and an uncontested fast break, but often their reward for a futile lunge was an uncontested lay-up by their opponent. Denied a fast break, they simply gave the ball to Luckett and then stood and watched while he, without benefit of a pick or a screen, shook loose of the two or three men guarding him and lofted a successful jump shot. To understand the extent to which Kolbe depended on Luckett, one has only to examine the team's scoring statistics. Often in a game Luckett would score fifty or more points while being triple-teamed, and his four teammates would manage only half that total against the other two defenders.

John Waldeyer, the brilliant Notre Dame coach who was in his early thirties, bore a striking resemblance in both style and girth to Orson Welles. He had blue eyes and a full-face blond beard. He spoke German fluently in a resonant voice, and his only interests seemed to be to dress in lederhosen for the annual Bridgeport Lions' Club Octoberfest Beer Festival and to guide the fortunes of his Notre Dame High School basketball team. He had always been fat, and in his youth never played organized sports. As manager and water boy for his high school football team he learned, sooner than most, to make his peace with the fact that, for him, sports would always be an intellectual pursuit rather than a physical activity. His interest in basketball grew and he read voluminously about it until, by the late 1960s when he became Notre Dame's basketball coach, he was one of the most technically knowledgeable coaches in the country. There was no defensive or offensive pattern he had not studied and memorized. His teams played a disciplined, white, suburban game commensurate with the school's student makeup during the 1960s and his own upbringing a decade earlier. The team ran intricate offensive patterns with numerous picks designed to spring players free for a perimeter jump shot or a backdoor lay-up—an offense particularly effective against Kolbe's over-aggressive defense. Notre Dame rarely executed a fast break, and on those occasions when they did it was more a spread-out military maneuver than a ghetto race.

Waldeyer's coaching philosophy changed a bit in the early 1970s as a greater number of ghetto-oriented whites matriculated at Notre Dame. By 1972 he was coaching less and allowing his players to exercise more individual freedom, for his starting team then was comprised of five ghetto players, four of whom were white. They had all played with or against Walter Luckett and most of his Kolbe teammates in their youth, although, naturally enough, they had always played in Luckett's shadow. It was not until their senior year at Notre Dame that these players had matured sufficiently to the point where, collectively, they might challenge Luckett's dominance of the game. They saw themselves as the new fast guns in town ready finally to try to overthrow the old order at the O.K. Corral. But they did not delude themselves. They knew that individually such a challenge to Luckett was beyond the range of their talents, if not their aspirations.

Frank Oleynick, Barry McLeod, Mark Gildea and Dennis McLaughlin were white, and Keith Lewis was black. They had all grown up in or very near one of the city's black ghettos, and all except Lewis were sullen boys. Lewis was a conservative guard. He seldom shot or initiated any action. He was personable, polite and well liked by most of the white Notre Dame students. His four teammates called him "The Oreo." Unlike Lewis, the four were not so universally loved by their fellow students, many of whom referred to them, not always behind their backs, as "nigger lovers." Gildea, of Irish extraction, had the perfect features, chiseled jaw and piercing blue eyes of a movie star. He had stringy, unkempt hair that fell below his shoulders. When he leaped for a rebound, hair flying and eyes blazing, he looked like a man possessed by demons. McLaughlin was also long-haired and wild-looking. At 6–1 he was the team's best leaper; he could dunk a basketball with either or both hands. He was of Irish and Spanish extraction and was raised in the same ghetto as Luckett.

McLeod and Oleynick, the team's top scorers, were first cousins and, more than that, inseparable friends. They had grown up in the foothills of Beardsley Terrace Apartments, the largest black ghetto in Bridgeport. McLeod, who averaged twenty-three points a game, was the team's playmaker, high scorer and point guard. He could dribble between his legs, pass behind his back and, at under six feet tall, dunk with either hand. In short, he could perform a host of playground maneuvers, most of which Coach Waldeyer frowned on in any but the most extreme emergencies. He was an unsmiling youth. His cousin, equally grim, at the time was not McLeod's equal as a jump shooter or ball handler. In fact, despite his twenty-two points per game scoring average, Frank Oleynick appeared to be the least physically talented of the four whites on the team. He was not as consistent a player as his cousin, nor as natural a leaper as Gildea and McLaughlin, nor as quick as any of the three. He had heavy legs severely knock-kneed. He drove to the basket with his head lowered like a charging bull. Oleynick was of Irish, Slovak and Hungarian heritage.

A few days before the Kolbe-Notre Dame game,

players from both teams confronted each other in the lobby of the Sacred Heart University gym, the site of their upcoming contest. Inside the gym a sparse crowd rooted desultorily for the SHU varsity basketball team. The smattering of cheers and applause from the gym was soon drowned out by the commotion in the lobby. Players from both Kolbe and Notre Dame, led by Luckett, Oleynick and McLeod, were taunting one another, at first good-naturedly and then more heatedly. They were being egged on by their friends and supporters, most of whom were black but whose allegiance was not racially motivated. In fact, there were as many blacks rooting for Oleynick and McLeod as there were for Luckett. The taunting got so out of hand that two policemen came out of the gym and threatened to disperse the youths. Cooler heads prevailed and the two sides calmed down. One of the witnesses to that scene, Donald Clemmons, a black former Notre Dame student who was a friend of Luckett and of Oleynick and McLeod, recalled that moment years later.

"Everybody from the projects was there," said Clemmons. "Kenny Knight, Ken Sumpter, Warren Blunt—all their friends. Luck started it all by woofin' at Frank and Barry. He was talkin' shit. 'I'm gonna bust your ass,' he says.

" 'Shit, you ain't,' says Barry.

" 'Shit, I am,' says Luck. 'I average more then you two combined.'

" 'So what?' says Frank. 'You the only guy on your team. You ain't got shit.'

" 'It don't matter,' says Luck, and then he turns sideways like he does, and puts one hand on his hip and with the other points a long finger at Frank and Barry.

'I'm tellin' you dudes, I dropped fifty on Harding and I be droppin' sixty on both of you.'

"Then Barry says real quiet, 'Yeah, but you ain't gonna win.'

" 'Shit, I ain't!' screams Luck in a girl's voice. 'Shiiit, I ain't! If I don't, I won't be able to show my face in the projects no more!'

"Then Sumpter steps between 'em to calm 'em down. By this time Frank and Barry be puffin' up their chests like they do, and Luck be staring 'em down through his eyebrows. Sumpt tries to separate them a little, and then he puts up his hands, like for quiet. You got to know Sumpt to see what I'm sayin'. Sumpter, he's a serious brother. He don't hardly smile. He wears these thick eyeglasses like a bookkeeper. Well, when he puts up his hands for quiet, everybody is so surprised they shut up. 'I just wanna say one thing,' says Sumpter. He pauses, then says in a low, steady voice like a prophet, 'If Luck outscores both Frank and Barry combined, Kolbe'll win. If he don't, Notre Dame'll win.' Then he walks away with everybody starin' after him like he was crazy."

When Notre Dame met Kolbe in November 1972 for bragging rights as the best high school basketball team in Bridgeport, almost 1200 people jammed themselves into Sacred Heart University's 800-seat gymnasium. From the moment the two teams came onto the court for their warm-up drills, the noise from the fans and cheerleaders was deafening. It never let up until the game was over.

At half-court during those warm-ups, Walter Luckett yelled across to Frank Oleynick and Barry McLeod.

"Look there," he said, pointing to a roped-off section of seats above the press table. "Every scout in the country is here. Providence is here. USC is here. Maryland. Seattle. Ohio U. Man, they all here! To see *me!* And I'm gonna turn it out." Then he laughed. "You boys better get yours, 'cause they be watching you, too."

Barry and Frank laughed, but when they turned back to their warm-ups, Barry said to Frank, "Don't let him get to you, man. He's just tryin' to rattle us."

As the two teams huddled with their respective coaches seconds before the game began, Barry McLeod glanced over his shoulder toward the Kolbe huddle. The players were bent over Lennie Lee, all except Luckett, who was standing up, hands on hips, looking into the stands. He scrutinized the scouts to see which colleges they represented, then turned toward his fans. They cheered and shouted his name. They stuck out pieces of paper and he autographed them. McLeod's mouth turned up in disgust. "Look at that," he said aloud. "Man, I know we gonna take 'em."

John Waldeyer, getting down laboriously on one knee, said to McLeod and his teammates, "Don't you worry about Luckett. Just hold the rest of his team down and we'll be all right. Luckett can't beat us by himself. Hell, what can he score, fifty?"

Walter Luckett scored forty-eight points that night. He made twenty of twenty-four field goal attempts. During the third period, with his team trailing by thirteen points, Luckett made nine of ten field goal attempts and four of five free throw attempts for a total of twenty-two points in an eight-minute quarter. Eight of those baskets were long, arching jump shots from at least 25 feet away. Each one fell through the center of the basket with such force and precision that the bottom of the net flounced up, like a woman's skirt, and wrapped itself around the metal rim. After each basket the referee had to call time out to untangle the net. When Luckett's streak ended at the close of the third quarter, his team was ahead by four points, and all the college scouts in attendance called it the greatest offensive scoring streak they had ever seen.

Luckett's brilliance in that game was not confined to long-range shooting. He also led both teams in rebounding and in assists, and in so doing almost completely overshadowed the fine, if mortal, performances of Barry McLeod and Frank Oleynick. McLeod, in particular, played a beautiful game. He single-handedly broke Kolbe's full-court press with such nonchalance, dribbling behind his back and through his legs, that from the stands he appeared to be threading his way through a row of folding chairs during practice. Once over half-court he pulled up at the top of the keyhole to examine the two teams spread out before him. Dribbling with one hand, he waved his teammates into position with the other prior to running an offensive play. Sometimes he simply pulled up short at the key and tossed in a form-perfect jump shot. At other times he did not even break stride after crossing half-court but continued straight toward the basket as if for a lay-up. When Kolbe's defenders collapsed around him, at the last possible second he glanced up at the basket and slipped the ball off his hip to Gildea or McLaughlin as nonchalantly as if discarding a piece of litter in a crowd.

Oleynick played almost as fine a game as his cousin, although since he was a forward, it was of a different kind. Oleynick did not handle the ball as much as McLeod; his job was primarily to rebound (he was two inches taller than McLeod) and score from the corner. His offensive moves were slower and more deliberate than his cousin's and, of necessity, more flamboyant. Whereas McLeod's basic moves were a long jump shot and a quick, strong drive straight to the basket, Oleynick tended to back in toward the basket left-right-left-right until finally, after several feints, he felt secure enough to turn on his man, whom he hoped was now out of position, and drive to the basket or else pull up and throw in a short jump shot. This night, however, Oleynick had difficulty shaking loose from his defender, Steve Cox, who was a good deal quicker than he. More than once Oleynick backed Cox toward the basket and whirled, only to find himself face-to-face with Cox. Frustrated, Oleynick often tried to knock him down, and was called with a number of charging fouls. Cox frustrated Oleynick in other ways. When Oleynick did not have the ball, Cox struck his face close to Oleynick's and called him names. He spat in Oleynick's face; Oleynick tried to ignore him, but Cox continued to taunt. Finally, during a time-out, Oleynick turned to McLeod in the team huddle and said, "Man, that brother be gettin' to me! He's always spittin' in my face! Dude makes me nervous!" McLeod twisted his mouth in disgust and said, "Oh, man, come on! Don't let him get you. Just do your thing."

The game's pace was furious. The two teams swapped leads and a host of unanswered points with such rapidity that its complexion changed every sixty seconds. Notre Dame up six, down four points fifty seconds later. The fans, yanked this way and that, were emotionally drained by the time the thirty-two-minute game was down to its last twenty-five seconds, the teams tied 90-all. Notre Dame had possession of the ball at half-court. McLeod, seemingly dribbling without a care, wove a tapestry through the Kolbe defense while the clock ticked away and the fans drew a breath in anticipation of the climax. With ten seconds left McLeod drove toward the basket. He slipped between three defenders, faked a handoff and threw up a hook shot. As the ball hit the backboard, the referee's whistle signaled a foul. The ball dropped in. McLeod sank his free throw to give Notre Dame a 93–90 lead with six seconds left to play.

Luckett took the ball on an out-of-bounds pass, dribbled across half-court and immediately lofted a long jump shot that fell cleanly through the net as the buzzer sounded. That basket cut Notre Dame's margin of victory to one point, 93–92. It earned Luckett his forty-seventh and forty-eighth points of the night, only one point shy of the combined totals of Barry McLeod and Frank Oleynick, who scored twenty-nine and twenty points respectively.

"That's Sumpter's pot of gold," said Don Clemmons years later. "He called it down to the point. Myself, I thought Kolbe shoulda won. Luck didn't shoot enough. Lots of people still think that. He coulda scored seventy. The dude's just too conservative. Now Frank and Barry, they played a wide-open game. One time, when Barry went through his legs on a dribble, I jumped up in the stands and started yelling. Shiiit, when I played for Waldeyer two years before, he usta take me outta the game when I went through my legs. Now, here's this little white dude turning it on and he don't say nothin'."

After the game most of the scouts milled around the Kolbe bench trying to get Walter Luckett's attention before he adjourned to the locker room. Only one scout bothered to walk over to the Notre Dame bench. He was a short, pudgy, elderly black man smoking a cigar. He was a coach at Morgan State College, an all-black school in Baltimore. He went over to Oleynick and McLeod, introduced himself and said to McLeod, "You can pat it pretty good, boy." He meant that McLeod was an adept ball handler. Then he said to both of the cousins, "You know, you boys could fit in pretty well at our school."

Meanwhile Don Clemmons had gone to the Kolbe locker room to console Luckett, who was crying and pounding his fist on the walls. "Damn! We lost! Damn! Damn! Damn!" Clemmons wanted to tell Luckett he should have taken more shots, but he did not. "I didn't want to come down on the dude," he said. Just then Marvin Barnes, a star basketball player at Providence College, walked into the locker room. He was there to recruit Luckett for Providence. "Brother, you got nothing to be sorry about," said Barnes. "You were great. That was the greatest high school game I ever saw." Howard Garfunkel was also in the Kolbe locker room. Garfunkel is famous in the East as a freelance scout of high school basketball players for any college that will pay him. His summer basketball camp for high school players in upstate New York is attended by many college and professional players as well as coaches. Garfunkel also publishes a tout sheet evaluating every decent high school player in the country. He has seen over 100 high school games a year for the past twenty years, and he said to Luckett, "That was the greatest high school game I ever saw, and your performance in it was the greatest single performance I've ever seen."

There were no scouts in the Notre Dame dressing room. There was only McLeod and Oleynick and Gildea and McLaughlin—the latter had scored twenty points mostly on feeds from McLeod—and Keith Lewis, who had scored sixteen points. They were slapping each other's palms, shouting, "We did it! We did it! We did it!" It was not just that they had beat Kolbe, but that finally, after all those years, they had emerged from Walter Luckett's shadow. It did not matter that Luckett had scored forty-eight points, that he had been brilliant. In fact, they had wanted Luckett to be brilliant, and still to beat him. McLeod, ordinarily a taciturn youth, was jubilant. He kept shouting, "Walt got the glory and we won the game!" Reminiscing today, McLeod says, "That was the greatest game I was ever in."

Walter Luckett agrees. "That was the greatest game I ever played in my life. I don't remember much specific, though, just that it was crazy, man. Everything I threw up went in, like a fuckin' dream. I made shots from half-court at both buzzers. But it wasn't just me. Frank and Barry were a bitch! Frank shot the shit out of the ball from the corner, and Barry, jeez, he went reckless abandon at the key. He was deadly. Deadly! All the college scouts saw 'em. When the scouts realized they wouldn't get me, they remembered Frank and Barry that night. In a lot of ways I was responsible for their careers."

three

Walter Luckett, Barry McLeod and Frank Oleynick were born and raised in Bridgeport, Connecticut, a decaying factory city of 200,000 people whose sole cultural event each year is a summer festival dedicated to the memory of a man whose only recorded words were: "There's a sucker born every minute." Phineas Taylor Barnum, father of the Barnum & Bailey Three-Ring Circus, was a native of Bridgeport. He was a master showman who made his fortune by always underestimating the intelligence of the American people. His most successful act was simply exhibiting two adult human beings, Tom Thumb and Lavinia Warren, who stood a shade over three feet tall. Barnum had the two get married and then billed them as the smallest couple in the world. He charged people admission to look at them. People flocked into the tent to stare and gasp in disbelief. Since they stared and gasped a bit too long to suit Barnum's taste, however, he had to devise a way to keep the crowd moving and the turnstiles turning more quickly. Above Tom Thumb and Lavinia Warren's heads he put a sign with an arrow. The sign read: "Next, See the Egress!" The crowd followed the arrow. Another sign read: "This Way to the Egress!" Still another read: "Approaching the Egress!" Finally, a sign over a door read: "At Last! The Egress!" The crowd went through the door and found themselves outside.

Bridgeport is the largest and poorest of a number of communities strung out directly northeast of New York City along the coast of Long Island Sound, together comprising affluent Fairfield County. Most of these communities—Westport, Darien, Greenwich—serve merely as bedrooms for transplanted New Yorkers who still work in the city. Bridgeport is the farthest from New York—48 miles away—and, as such, suffers both because of its distance from and proximity to the largest city in the world. Few Bridgeporters commute to New York, for it is 1½ hours by car or train. They find it more convenient to make their living in one of the factories in their own city. Nor do they look to New York for their amusements. Residents are primarily blue-collar workers who cannot really afford New York's many pleasures, most of which they regard suspiciously as more than slightly decadent. Bridgeporters take their amusements at home, in overtime at the Brass Shop and at the city's annual Barnum Festival Parade. Despite being inhabitants of the largest city in Fairfield County, and in the state for that matter, Bridgeporters are basically of a rural mentality, in contrast to those inhabitants of the small towns to the southwest who are decidedly urbane. The latter are primarily professionals—corporate lawyers and executives and more creative Madison Avenue types—for whom a forty-minute train ride even on the not always reliable Penn Central is a small price to pay for living in suburban luxury less than an hour from their offices. Their salaries and proximity to New York make it possible for them to look to the city for their amusements—dinner, dancing, the theater—their urbanity demands something in addition to the annual Barnum Festival Parade. They would no more think of going to Bridgeport to be entertained than a Broadway producer would think of premiering a potentially successful play in Bridgeport rather than on Broadway. In fact, there is an old show business axiom: "After New York, everything else is Bridgeport."

When the producers of the film *Johnny, We Hardly Knew Ye,* a biography of John F. Kennedy as a youthful politician in Boston, were searching for a city that most resembled Boston in the 1940s, they discovered Bridgeport in 1976. Bridgeporters were understandably proud of the producers' choice, but not so understandably were oblivious to the irony of that choice. Bridgeport still resembles a factory city from the 1940s. Its skyline is a forest of smokestacks, each emitting a palpable haze of various autumn hues. Its soot-stained brick factories, baroque office buildings and once stately Victorian homes that are now sagging three-family tenements are only rarely interspersed with a nondescript modern building which, in Bridgeport, seems less a sign of urban renewal than a glaring anachronism. But downtown Bridgeport is in a never-ending state of urban renewal. Old buildings are demolished, leaving behind gaping holes littered with bricks and broken bottles. The holes remain untouched for years until finally a new building emerges. Within a short time that building will grow soot-stained too, so what once looked out of place now blends easily into the cityscape. The corridors in the new railroad station smell of urine; the new courthouse was called an "architectural monstrosity" before it was completed;

and the city's largest shopping mall suffers such a rash of muggings in its parking lots that now it is all but deserted at night, except for the dozens of security guards keeping in touch on their walkie-talkies as they trail roaming gangs of youths.

Ever since the turn of the century, this city has been a way station for the overflow of European immigrants who disembarked at Riker's Island in New York. They moved northeast into Connecticut and stopped at Bridgeport, where many factories held promise of fulfillment of the American Dream. They worked hard, saved their pennies and cherished the hope that, for them, Bridgeport would never be home but rather a place to leave someday. After a generation or two they did leave, migrating to a home in the suburbs. They left the city to others, like themselves, who somehow through weakness or sloth, madness or despair, or maybe just the quirky hand of fate, could not even navigate that first simple step toward the American Dream. They were left behind to work in the factories, get laid off, start small businesses, watch them fail, return again to the factories where, in the 1950s and 1960s, they were forced to work alongside a new wave of immigrants, Puerto Ricans and Cubans and blacks from the South. Today the blacks and the Spanish-speaking peoples of Bridgeport make up over 30 percent of the city's population and over 70 percent of its school population. They live near those second- and third-generation European Americans in housing projects that had once been ethnic ghettos of two- and three-story Victorian houses but today bear not the slightest resemblance to what they once were.

* * *

There are three major black ghettos in Bridgeport: the P. T. Barnum Housing Project in the south end, Father Panik Village in the east end, and the Beardsley Terrace Apartments in the north end. The south end had once been home for the city's substantial Hungarian population until the arrival of great numbers of blacks and the building of the P. T. Barnum Project, at which time most of those Hungarian-Americans moved further south to the suburb of Fairfield. P. T., as it is called by its residents, is nothing more than a number of square, faceless brick buildings spread over a desolate landscape. There are no trees or grass, just the buildings and the streets and the parking lots and the intermittent paved areas and, surrounding the entire project like a moat, a vast open stretch of broken bottles, bricks and assorted debris. That open stretch isolates the project and its inhabitants from the few old homes and small businesses that lie beyond its borders and imagination. P. T. is a stagnant, spiritless place where every other car is on cinder blocks and the outdoor basketball courts are deserted even at midafternoon on a sunny day. Nothing is stirring. A dog sniffs garbage. An old man squats protectively before his pile of junk, sprung mattresses and rusted car fenders. Two policemen, one black and the other white, patrol the streets, twirling their nightsticks and holding tight to the leashes of their German Shepherd attack dogs.

Father Panik Village is named after Slovakian priest Father Stephen Panik, who was instrumental in establishing an eastern European settlement in the east end of Bridgeport during the 1930s. Most of the ancestors of those Czech, Slovak and Polish immigrants have long since deserted the area, leaving it to the blacks and Spanish when they moved east to the suburb of Stratford. The Panik, as it is called, takes in both the newer brick apartments similar to those in P. T. and the older three- and four-family homes that once belonged to the ethnics. Unlike P. T., which is simply a small island in the south end, the Panik encompasses not only the brick buildings that make up the village itself, but also the entire east end of the city. The Panik *is* the east end, a city within a city, a congested area of apartments, tenements, stores and people. Because of its high density and monolithic nature, the Panik was particularly susceptible to violence during the 1960s riots, when most white merchants were burned out of the area. Those who remained spawned a new architecture—bricked-in windows, iron gates—"Riot Renaissance." The Panik is still a seething area of crime, drugs, prostitution and violence that erupts without warning. Policemen, white or black, do not walk through the Panik. They ride in patrol cars with their attack dogs in the back.

The Beardsley Terrace Apartments were so named because of their proximity to Beardsley Park, a lush green haven about three miles to the south. Beardsley Park has a zoo, baseball diamonds, tennis courts, hockey rink, swimming lake and fishing stream. It has picnic areas that are crowded each summer weekend with blacks from the Beardsley Terrace Apartments.

The Terrace, as it is called, is just that—a cluster of high-rise brick buildings perched on a plateau overlooking the north end of the city. Around and below the Terrace are the modest homes of blacks and some whites, mostly Italian-Americans not as successful as others of their nationality who fled north to the suburb of Trumbull. The Terrace is two blocks of concrete and bricks and pavement containing 10,000 people. It does not look much different from P. T. Its buildings appear just as desolate, although taller. Its streets are also littered with dead cars. But whereas P. T. is isolated from the surrounding community, the Terrace is very much a part of the residential area of modest homes that begins across the street. The Terrace is surrounded by grass and trees, and from its windows residents can see blacks and whites watering their lawns. Many of those small homeowners once lived in the Terrace. Unlike P. T. and the Panik, the Terrace is a ghetto whose residents can see the possibility for escape. It has given them hope. On a summer's day young mothers push baby carriages along the sidewalks, nodding and chatting with other mothers as they pass. Children play in the street. Men bury their heads under the hoods of their cars and try to repair them. Boys play basketball on the paved court.

At night the Terrace is even more alive, like a summer festival in a small town. The streets and walks are crowded with strollers. People lean against parked cars and pass wine bottles back and forth as they watch a men's basketball game being played under lights. The men's basketball league is only one of the many organized sporting leagues run at the Terrace. The court is pulsing with the slap of flesh, the shrill whistles and groans of the players, while from the sidelines the fans cheer and applaud and laugh. Occasionally, from the darkness of the court, there is an angry shout, a curse and the sound of broken glass. Like P. T. and the Panik, the Terrace is not free from violence, but its causes are different. P. T.'s violence springs from despair, the Panik's from hatred. Violence in the Terrace has more logical roots—a stolen radio, someone else's wife, tarnished pride. The police do not often patrol through the Terrace, partly because their presence is less a deterrent than an incentive to violence, partly because the Terrace, as the most organized of the city's ghettos, does much to police itself.

Angelo Nocciolli, a second-generation Italian-American with six children, could pass for a character out of a Mario Puzo novel. He is gaunt and grizzled. His hooked nose seems determined to meet his upturned chin. Some of his teeth are missing. He has a sinister mustache and a light stubble on his sunken cheeks. Often he dresses entirely in black. In Bridgeport he is known as "The Godfather," which he is, to Walter Luckett, Jr. He first met his godson fifteen years ago, when he was a fireman on the east side of Bridgeport near Father Panik Village.

One winter day after a snowstorm, Mr. Nocciolli was standing outside the firehouse passing time with his co-workers, all of whom were white, when he saw a skinny black youth about nine years old struggling through the high drifts. The snow was up to the boy's thighs and he was having great difficulty managing the oil can he was going to get filled with kerosene at the corner store. Something about the boy caught Mr. Nocciolli's attention. He noticed the boy was wearing sneakers, one green and one purple. He felt sorry for him. He called out and waved. The boy did not respond to the tough-looking white man. Each day at the same time the boy would pass by with the oil can, and each day Mr. Nocciolli would wave and call out. One day the boy waved back. Finally the boy mustered enough courage to come over and talk to the fireman. Before the boy left, the fireman gave him money to buy donuts. The boy returned each day, and he and the fireman became friends. Still the boy was reticent around the other firemen, whom he sensed did not approve of the odd pair. The boy was right. Whenever he left, Mr. Nocciolli's co-workers would kid him about his friendship with "the skinny nigger." They asked why he befriended the youth, and Mr. Nocciolli was not able to give them an answer.

One day after work, Mr. Nocciolli stopped off at a neighborhood bar for a drink. He saw the boy with three younger boys and a man, who must surely be their father. He introduced himself to the father and bought him a drink. The two men sat at the bar drinking and talking for a long time, and during the course of their conversation they discovered they had much in common. Mr. Luckett told Mr. Nocciolli that his sister had married an Italian-American, the owner of a black nightclub in Bridgeport, and although the marriage had not worked out, he implied it was more his sister's fault than his brother-in-law's. He was partial to Italians, Mr. Luckett said, and then, much to the fireman's surprise, he began to speak to him in fluent Italian. Both men also had large families and were devoted to them. Mr. Luckett had been one of eight children himself, and when his mother had expressed fear that the Luckett name would die out with this generation, he told her not to worry, he would have plenty of sons to carry on the name. When she was dying and he brought his four sons to her bedside, she looked up and said, "I didn't mean this many!" He promised her that his sons would be good boys and would never cause any problems.

He watched his sons closely. At the time he met Mr.

Nocciolli he was working as a laborer for a construction firm and, whenever possible, he would bring his boys with him to his job on the back of his flatbed truck. He feared for them in the ghetto. He wanted to protect them from ghetto evils, which was why he even took his sons to the bar with him. "He took his kids everywhere," Mr. Nocciolli said years later. "He lived through his kids. He loved all kids, in fact. His house was always open to them, black or white. He and his wife would feed them, even when they had no money. When I first met him he had no favorites, not even Walter, who was his oldest."

Because of his affection for boys, who were inclined to be a source of trouble in the ghetto, Mr. Luckett was looked on as the unofficial goodwill ambassador between the black and white communities in Bridgeport during the tumultuous mid-1960s. He had no prejudices. His home was filled, day and night, with people of every color and nationality. At any moment one might hear three different languages being spoken at once. Mr. Luckett spoke seven languages, among them Italian, Yiddish and Polish. Much to his sons' embarrassment, he delighted in walking into a strange ethnic bar, sitting down and then turning to his neighbor and conversing with him in his native tongue.

Mr. Luckett was particularly well liked by most whites, even more so than by blacks. He had an affinity for the former he somehow could not stir up for the latter. He could pass for white himself. His skin was the color of butter. He was an emaciated man with spidery limbs and a rubbery, expressive face that was not just lined but deeply furrowed as if its possessor had lost a great deal of weight too quickly. When he spoke passionately, which was often, his lips peeled apart like an open wound. His voice came out as if sifted through a throat full of gravel, the voice of a much more substantial man. His eyes were as blue as Paul Newman's, his nose as straight and fine. He told his sons that his father had been a white man who lived in Fairfield. Mr. Luckett had only seen him once in his life. He and his eight brothers and sisters (mostly sisters) had been raised in Bridgeport by their mother, a dark-skinned woman. Unlike many blacks of his generation who had come to Bridgeport from the South, Mr. Luckett was a native of the city. He spoke with neither a ghetto nor a southern accent. As a youth he was quick-witted and intelligent. He skipped two grades in grammar school, then quit high school at the age of twelve to take a job in a meat market to support his mother and the family. He would hold many jobs over the years, most of which he mastered quickly, grew bored with and then either quit or lost because of indifference.

He was not a sullen drinker, one who grew silent and brooding as his head inclined closer and closer to the bar. Mr. Luckett grew expansive as he drank. He did not drink to dull his perceptions, already dulled by reality's harsh glow, but to brighten them. With each drink he became more animated as reality was muted, dissolved, and he was left only with his perceptions, now cleanly defined, bolder than life and seemingly within his grasp. "Walter Sr. always dreamed in his mind what he would like to be," said Mr. Nocciolli years after their first meeting. "But somehow he could never act it out. As he got older he acted it out through his kids, especially Walter, Jr."

As they drank that first night, Mr. Luckett confided his dreams to Mr. Nocciolli. They concerned his sons.

He wanted great things for them in life, he said. He was sure they were all exceptional boys who would fulfill his dreams if only he could get them out of the ghetto. Then, in a burst of self-pity, Mr. Luckett bemoaned his inability to make a decent living for his family in Bridgeport. Mr. Nocciolli snapped at him: "Don't cry to me. It's no easier for me than you. I got six kids. I can see you like to take it easy. You like to take a drink, too." Then Mr. Nocciolli said that if Mr. Luckett was really that concerned about his sons, he would see what he could do. He had a friend, George Fasolo, who ran the Archbishop Sheehan Center in downtown Bridgeport. The Sheehan Center, named after former Bridgeport Bishop Lawrence J. Sheehan, was a recreational center not unlike the city's many boys' clubs, but with some noticeable differences. Unlike the boys' clubs, each of which drew from one particular section of the city, the Sheehan Center drew from the entire city and its surrounding suburbs. Only a very few of the Sheehan Center's youths were black. Most were white, either tough inner-city youths like Dennis McLaughlin or the sons of doctors and lawyers who had been raised in the city, benefited from its toughening powers and then, with affluence, fled to the suburbs. Now they worried about the effects of the suburbs on their sons every bit as much as Mr. Luckett, and others like him, worried about the effect of ghetto life on their sons. The latter feared their sons were going hard; the former feared theirs were going soft, and to impede that process they sent them back into the city, to the Sheehan Center, where it was hoped they would be roughed up just enough, but certainly not too much, certainly not as much as Mr. Luckett's boys would be in the ghetto.

Most of the youths in Bridgeport's boys' clubs were poor and black, and their parents, when they had more than one, were indifferent to their sons' upbringing, in contrast to Mr. Luckett. Their sons ran wild on the streets and were tamed only slightly inside the boys' clubs, whose primary attraction for them was an indoor basketball court they could use for a membership fee of one dollar a year. They played wearing street clothes, jeans and hard-soled shoes. They did not bring towels or a change of underwear because they did not expect to take a shower. The Sheehan Center charged five dollars a year for a membership card, and its youths were not allowed on the basketball court unless they were properly dressed in shorts and sneakers.

The boys' clubs, though generally newer buildings than the Sheehan Center, were dirty, worn-down and poorly organized in comparison. The Sheehan Center was kept spotless by George Fasolo, who ran it with the same philosophy and discipline that Vince Lombardi ran the Green Bay Packers. Fasolo did not hesitate to expel a youth for a transgression that seemed harmless enough but which cost the offending youth the princely sum of five dollars. His reasoning was simple: to discourage more daring transgressions, he made sure that the punishment always exceeded the crime. Fasolo was a tough Italian-American in his mid-forties. He had a generous paunch and short, steely gray hair. He was not an unkind man, but neither was he a sentimentalist. In dealing with a great many youths of various backgrounds, he found it easier to meet them on an objective rather than subjective plane. He was an egalitarian who treated everyone the same, lawyers' sons from the suburbs and blacks. The boys had to adjust to his way of doing things, which was rooted in a simpler time and a simpler place. Fasolo came to Bridgeport in 1962 from Farmington, Connecticut, a small farming community in the middle of the state. He brought with him small-town disciplines which were more easily assimilated by the Sheehan Center's ethnic and suburban whites than by the ghetto blacks, which further explained why so few of the latter joined the Center.

When George Fasolo became the executive director of the Sheehan Center, he started a scrapbook, now grown to three, to keep track of his and the Center's achievements. That third red book, an imitation leather photo album from the five-and-dime, chronicles the years 1965 to 1967. Each newspaper clipping in it is neatly arranged on the page and covered by an acetate sheet. Fasolo takes great pride in these books and the events they chronicle. There is a story about five youths arrested after they dared to steal metal rain gutters from the Center. There is the engagement picture of Miss Magda Emily Morejon, an employee of the Center, and Servando de la Cruz of Cuba. There is a picture of some boys getting on a bus for a trip to Yankee Stadium; they are white, as are most of the youths pictured in this scrapbook. There is a story about Fasolo's election to the presidency of the Fairfield County Pop Warner Midget Football Conference. There is a photograph of the 1967 Sheehan Center Trojans, winners of the annual Boys' Clubs of Bridgeport City Open Basketball Tournament. The latter shows eleven boys in uniform between the ages of twelve and thirteen, lined up along a wall over which hangs a large crucifix. Most of the boys look alike: long-legged, crew cut, serious. All but one is white. Standing at the end of the line, wearing a plaid sport jacket and a skinny tie, is George Fasolo, looking like a diminutive Spiro Agnew. Years later, viewing that photograph, he points out each of the boys and gives a capsule commentary on the turn of their lives since the picture was taken. "That's Dennis McLaughlin," he says, "who went on to college in San Antonio." He points to another boy, now a policeman. And another, who is dead. He shakes his head sadly. He stops at the image of the only black youth in the photograph. The boy is looking up into the camera with a smile.

"Walter came into our lives in 1965," says Fasolo. "His father brought him to us because he was worried about him. He was going to a ghetto grammar school and, although he wasn't a bad boy, he was getting a smart mouth on him. It was winter. I remember he was wearing sneakers, one green and one purple. I took him in because of Angie Nocciolli. He was just an average kid. He had no great potential then. He was just one of a great mesh of kids, rich and poor, at the Center. He knew his way around a basketball court even then, although he couldn't shoot very well. I used to yell at him, 'Walter, don't shoot! Just rebound!' He would blow the easiest lay-ups."

Like Mr. Nocciolli, George Fasolo soon found himself taking a special interest in Walter Luckett, Jr., although to this day he is not sure why. Other whites would be drawn to Walter Luckett when it became obvious, a few years later, that his basketball talent was something special, but George Fasolo was drawn to him before he exhibited even a hint of that talent. Maybe it was his smile, he says in retrospect. It was completely without guile. In that scrapbook picture Walter is looking up, smiling, his throat muscles straining and his mouth open. He looks like a newborn bird in a nest. When Walter Luckett first came to the Sheehan Center he was as innocent and blank as any newborn waiting only to be fed by others. More than any black youth of his generation, more even than any white, Walter Luckett trusted white adults. In fact, Walter trusted whites like George Fasolo and Angelo Nocciolli as much as he did black adults.

It was that trusting look of his, that innocence, that probably prompted Fasolo to take a special interest in Walter. After basketball practice, Fasolo, who was the Trojans' coach, would drive the youngster back to his home in the east end. Walter would always tell Fasolo to drop him off at the best kept house in the east end, as if implying that that was his home. It wasn't. "He didn't want me to see where he really lived," says Fasolo. "It preyed on my mind. I felt sorry for him." Fasolo's pity for Walter was less a result of his deprived economic circumstances than of the effect that deprivation was having on the youngster's psyche. It was apparent to Fasolo that although Walter seemed to be blending smoothly into the Center's way of life after only a short while, he seemed inordinately enamored of the life-styles of his more affluent teammates. "Walter saw those rich kids at the Sheehan Center and he aspired to be like them," says Fasolo. "There was no way, what with his father and all. But he never could see that as a kid. Those whites really impressed him, and they in turn were impressed by him. Walter had a way of drawing whites to him. He was a helluva diplomat for the Sheehan Center."

Eventually Walter Luckett's desire to be like his white teammates would have a disruptive effect on his life, though at first it only prompted him to try to fit into the Center's flow. "Oh, he was always a cocky kid," says Fasolo, "but there were never any ego problems with him at first. He just floated along with us. We taught him to do well in school. Whenever he had a problem we told him to pray. We told him he should strive to be a part of society."

Three years after he first entered the Center, Walter Luckett, at the age of thirteen, began to cause Fasolo some problems by showing off in front of his teammates. He tried to take liberties with Fasolo and, when he was rebuked, he sulked. Fasolo told Mr. Nocciolli that Walter had begun to "dog it." What had happened simply was that after three years Walter had begun to despair of ever becoming a part of that society Fasolo had urged him to join. He still lived in the ghetto, a place he was too ashamed to have any of his white friends see. He felt he had been deceived. He turned to militant blacks in his own community and fell briefly under their influence. "It wasn't a big thing," says Mr. Nocciolli. "Walter was always a good kid. But I told Walt, Sr., about it anyway. He got very upset. He jumped all over the boy. I told him it wasn't that serious, that he had to let the boy grow on his own. But he wouldn't listen. He was always terrified the boy would go 'black' on him. Whenever Walter, Jr., disagreed with him over the slightest thing, the whole family would be all over the boy. It was hard on him. In the Sheehan Center he could act white. He could be a good guy. He could act loving, kind and humble. But when he went back to the arena, those things were taken as a sign of weakness by blacks. He had to act tough, cool. We always explained to him the right way he should act in the white world, but we never saw the way he acted back in the ghetto. With me, though, he was always respectful. No matter how old he was, he was never embarrassed to introduce me to blacks as his godfather."

Walter's show of petulance coincided with the emergence of his basketball talent. At twelve he had excelled as a Little League pitcher and Pop Warner football player, and at thirteen he stood above all the basketball players his age in the city. He had grown to almost six feet. He regularly scored thirty points for the Sheehan Center Trojans. When his team won the Boys' Clubs City Open Basketball Tournament in 1967, Walter was unanimously picked the event's Most Valuable Player. "He was fantastic in all sports," says Fasolo. "He could have been great in anything. And he had this tremendous charisma."

Talent and personality drew people to Walter Luckett. Whites, like Fasolo, saw hope for him because of that personality. He was the kind of youth they felt could be saved from the ghetto and become a responsible member of society. Furthermore, in the Sheehan Center's atmosphere, he would be proof that ghetto blacks and suburban whites were compatible after all and that there was hope for American society. That was why Fasolo referred to Walter as a "helluva diplomat" for the Center. Walter would draw to the Center those white sons of suburban doctors and lawyers who wanted their youngsters to experience inner-city blacks—not the typical hardened blacks of the ghetto, but blacks like Walter Luckett, who was by no means typical of the ghetto.

Other whites were attracted to Walter for selfish reasons. They saw in his emerging talent a force they could use for personal gain. Some wanted merely to bask in his athlete's glow. Others had more pragmatic motives, wanting to influence his choice of high school and then college, which at the very least would enhance their own prestige as scouts of young basketball talent. Ghetto blacks were not much different than many of those whites. They saw in Walter's talent a force they could use to lend prestige to the black community and, like those whites, they were oblivious to the effect this use might have on Walter Luckett himself. They began to pressure him to quit the predominantly white Sheehan Center and join one of the city's many black-dominated boys' clubs, particularly the Middle Street Boys' Club.

The Middle Street Boys' Club was located in the heart of the city, across from a deserted railroad station whose parking lot was used at night by cruising homosexuals and prostitutes. It was the oldest and most decrepit of all the city's boys' clubs, but also the one with the most prestigious basketball reputation. It was a soot-stained red-brick building with a boxy, low-ceilinged gym on the third floor. One side of that gym's boundary line was simply a brick wall, and any ball bouncing off that wall was still in play. The building had been built shortly after the turn of the century, when the game still revolved around the center jump after each basket and when the ball itself had white stitches like a football. The gym was dark and close, and its floors were warped, like the one in which Dr. Naismith nailed up that first peach basket. For years it had been the site of some of the best basketball games in the city, played by touring professional and semiprofessional teams such as the Original Celtics and The House of David Five, the latter a team supposedly of orthodox Jews but actually comprised of white gentiles. Only in the last fifteen or so years had the Middle Street Boys' Club been taken over by blacks. In fact, by the time Walter Luckett was thirteen, only two whites regularly played at the club: Frank Oleynick and Barry McLeod. At the time the club still had a reputation for producing the most talented players in the city. The Sheehan Center, in comparison, had only mediocre players, except of course for Walter Luckett, and yet they regularly trounced the city's boys' club teams, including Middle Street.

"Middle Street had all the most talented players in the city, except for Walter," says Fasolo. "But as great as they were, we'd always kill them. They never saw a one-three-one zone defense before. We were too organized for them. Of course, if we ran or tried to go one-on-one with them, they'd blow us out of the gym."

Under Fasolo's tutelage, Walter Luckett learned to play the kind of deliberate, disciplined game known in the city as "a white, suburban game." His team brought the ball over half-court deliberately, set up their offense and then executed a play. They played a variety of zone defenses that allowed their often less talented players to help one another out. As a coach, Fasolo broke down the game of basketball to its simplest parts—shooting, rebounding, dribbling, passing, and so on. He assigned each player only those parts of the game at which he excelled. By hiding his players' deficiencies, Fasolo's team became greater than the sum of each player's parts. This benefited the team at the expense of individual talents. Since each player executed only those parts of the game at which he excelled, his strong points grew stronger while his weaknesses atrophied.

At first Walter Luckett could only rebound. Then, at thirteen, he could rebound and shoot long-range jump shots. He was so accurate a long-range shooter, in fact, that Fasolo devised plays by which Walter could get off his shots behind a teammate's screen. It was all so easy for Walter that he seldom bothered to penetrate the other team's defense for a lay-up. Nor did he handle the ball often or play a tight man-to-man defense. In fact, no one player at the Sheehan Center played a complete game by himself, but only in consort with his teammates. The Trojans played in harmony with each player contributing his specialty, much in the same way that the Portland Trail Blazers utilized their talents in beating the Philadelphia 76ers for the National Basketball Association championship in 1977.

Teams at the Middle Street Boys' Club played a black, inner-city game. Each player tried to master all aspects of the game which became, for him, an opportunity to satisfy the demands of his ego. Often those demands were satisfied at the expense of the team. Centers tried to dribble the ball behind their back, and kicked it out of bounds. Small guards, such as Frank Oleynick and Barry McLeod, drove through heavy traffic toward the basket in an attempt to dunk the ball, which was more often than not swatted away by the opposition's center. (After a game in which Luckett played against Oleynick, Fasolo grabbed Walter by the back of his neck and shook him good-naturedly. He told him he was proud of the fine, disciplined game he had played, in contrast to Oleynick's undisciplined game. Then Fasolo said, as an afterthought, "You know, Walter, you shoulda been white. That other one, Oleynick, he shoulda been black." That perception made an impression on Fasolo, and from then on, whenever Walter did something that pleased him, Fasolo would grab him by the back of the neck, shake him and say, "Walter, I'm tellin' you, you shoulda been white and that other one shoulda been black.")

No aspect of the game was off limits to any player on a Middle Street team. Eventually this would benefit their careers, but it was detrimental to team play at the moment. The team became less than the sum of each players' parts, just as the Philadelphia 76ers were in 1977. Thus whenever the Middle Street team played the Sheehan Center Trojans the result was as predictable as the Portland-Philadelphia series in 1977.

Walter Luckett's career at the Sheehan Center reached its zenith in 1967 when his team went undefeated and he was named the Center's "Boy of the Year." In one of his last games for the Center before he received that award, he scored fifty-nine points against Ridgefield High School's junior varsity team, also undefeated. It was the first time Walter had played a game outside the city. He was awed by Ridgefield, a wealthy Fairfield County commuter town noted for its pristine colonial mansions. Driving past one such mansion with its sprawling lawns and thick maple trees, Walter turned to George Fasolo and asked, without wonder, "Is that a house?" It was, said Fasolo, and only then was Walter intimidated. But he was not intimidated by Ridgefield's players, some two and three years his senior. He played so brilliantly, in fact, that Dr. Peter Yanity, an Ohio University alumnus and recruiter who saw the game, immediately began to seek Walter Luckett for Ohio University, even though Walter was not yet in high school.

Dr. Yanity, a dentist, is white. He is short and portly, with steel gray hair and a twitch in his left eye. The twitch is most evident when he's nervous. Unlike Fasolo, who is a long-standing friend, Dr. Yanity is less a disciplinarian than a diplomat. He says of Walter Luckett, "That first time I saw him he was outstanding. He was very mannerly. He showed great confidence on the court. He was a leader who dominated, and he knew it. George had done a wonderful job with that team. They were motivated, organized and well-disciplined, which was very unusual for such young kids, especially ones coming from their background." Dr. Yanity would follow Walter's career from the Sheehan Center through high school. Ultimately, he was responsible for Walter's choosing to attend Ohio University over such prestigious basketball schools as UCLA, Maryland and Notre Dame.

The day after that Ridgefield game the Trojans held a practice at the Center. During this practice an event occurred that would affect the course of Walter Luckett's life, for better or worse. Walter was feeling especially proud of himself after his performance the night before, and so, during a drill, he asked Fasolo if he could get a drink of water. Fasolo said no. Walter asked again. Fasolo said no again, and reminded Walter it was not his custom to let players get a drink during practice. Walter pleaded with him, but Fasolo held fast. "You're no different than anyone else on this team," he said. When Fasolo was not looking, Walter snuck over to the water fountain and got a drink. Fasolo caught him. "I told him to get out of the gym," says Fasolo today. "I told him he was off the team. His mouth dropped open. He couldn't believe it. It wasn't just the water incident, though. It was a culmination of irritating things like that. For instance, when he first came to the Center, Walter was always early for practice. He'd hop on his rickety bike and be the first one there. Now he was showing up late. I had to put my foot down."

Although Mr. Nocciolli generally agreed with his

friend's disciplinary measures, this time he came to Walter's defense. "George had done wonderful things for Walter," says Mr. Nocciolli today. "He had taught him to wear a shirt and tie. He had given Walter an opportunity to play on an organized team for the first time in his life. But still, George didn't understand the boy sometimes. Especially about his being late. I explained to George that no one gave Walter a ride to practice. I told him my kid was never late because I drove him to practice every day."

Fasolo remained adamant, however. He pointed out that Walter had had no difficulty being on time before he became a "star" and said he would not tolerate such behavior now. "Walter couldn't believe what was happening to him," says Fasolo. "He called to apologize to me. I told him he had to apologize to the whole team. It was their decision whether or not to take him back. Walter came to my office, where I made him wait for me from 2:45 P.M. to 5:45 P.M. Then I let him apologize to the team and they took a vote on whether or not to take him back. They all wanted him back, of course—the vote was unanimous—but I told Walter it was only 7–6 in his favor. He was stunned. I think that incident was a turning point in Walter's life. His behavior really improved after that."

While Walter Luckett was waiting in George Fasolo's office for three hours that day, he thought about his decision to apologize to Fasolo and the team. Of course the choice had not been entirely his own. He had called Mr. Nocciolli and asked his advice. Mr. Nocciolli told him it would be best to apologize. It was the right decision, Walter thought. He had reaped many benefits from his association with the Sheehan Center, George

Fasolo and Mr. Nocciolli, benefits that were far more substantial than any notoriety he had earned through his basketball talent but which, he felt, were earned nevertheless only because of that talent.

Mr. Nocciolli and George Fasolo had gotten Walter transferred from his ghetto grammar school to St. Augustine's grammar school in downtown Bridgeport. St. Augustine's, taught by priests and nuns, was a peaceful if rigidly disciplined haven in contrast to his former drug-infested school. Each morning he put on a shirt and tie and sport jacket before going off to St. Augustine's. That outfit gave him pleasure. Before he was admitted to St. Augustine's, however, Walter, who was not raised a Catholic, had to convert to Roman Catholicism. He took lessons. A few days before he was to be baptized, he asked Mr. Nocciolli to stand up for him. Nocciolli said he would. Walter was thirteen, and that gesture would endear Mr. Nocciolli to him for the rest of his life. Walter grew to love him. Mr. Nocciolli was without guile, the most unprejudiced human being Walter would ever meet. Mr. Nocciolli's father, an immigrant who could barely speak English, had had blacks at his dinner table for as long as his son could remember, and now that son, Angelo Nocciolli, had become godfather to a black youth.

Walter Luckett treated his godfather with a respect he reserved for no one else, not even his own father. He never failed to introduce Mr. Nocciolli to blacks and whites as his godfather, and he never failed to be suffused with pleasure at the mention of those words. Blacks responded to Mr. Nocciolli with the utmost respect, as did whites to Walter upon hearing of the relationship between the two. Even those white firemen who had called

Walter "nigger" behind his back became deferential to him now. They loved to share in his basketball exploits as if they were partly their own. Mr. Nocciolli told Walter that not a day went by at the station in which someone did not ask, "How's your godson?" He did not tell Walter, however, that often that question was tinged with sarcasm.

Mr. Nocciolli and George Fasolo had also helped get the entire Luckett family transferred from the east end ghetto to the Green Apartments, a racially mixed housing complex high on a hill in downtown Bridgeport. The Green Apartments were not a ghetto in the strict sense of the word. They housed blacks, Puerto Ricans, Portuguese, Italians and other of the city's poorest white ethnics. There was even a contingent of the Hell's Angels Motorcycle Club ensconced in a building near the Apartments. Those Angels, known locally as The Huns, occupied the entire building. They parked their gleaming bikes in slanting military formation the length of an entire block. The Huns had a machine gun mounted on a turret on the building's roof. They did not bother much with the blacks of the area, but they did have a running war with another motorcycle club, The Grateful Dead, and with the area's Puerto Rican and Portuguese population.

If the Green Apartments were not the suburbs, still, despite its random violence, they were not strictly one of the city's ghettos either. Their residents were burdened with none of the ghetto dwellers' claustrophobic sense of despair, of being trapped and isolated by natural or artificial barriers. The Green Apartments were a homogeneous mix of the city's nationalities who did not feel cordoned off from their neighbors. However, this also prevented them from developing any strong sense of identity as did ghetto blacks, who found in their isolation and monolithic nature a strength and unity and pride they would not have had in the Green Apartments. Such identity was thrust on ghetto residents, not by choice but by necessity, just as dignity is thrust on a man dying of cancer. Because blacks in the Green Apartments had options open to them denied ghetto blacks, they tended to be less unified, less militant, less prone to violence, and economically better off. This prompted ghetto residents to denigrate them for being deficient in black pride. In fact, even two of Walter Luckett's white contemporaries, Frank Oleynick and Barry McLeod, who lived in the foothills of Beardsley Terrace, used to tease Walter in shrill, sissy voices for living in "The Pink Apartments" or "The Punk Apartments."

The realization that he had been responsible for his family's escape from the ghetto to the Green Apartments pleased Walter Luckett, Jr. It pleased him because he could see it pleased his father. Mr. Luckett had instilled in all his sons a strong familial, rather than ethnic, pride. He had preached that it was each son's duty to help fulfill the family's destiny. And it thrilled Walter to know that he was finally contributing to that destiny.

Looking back on those years recently, Walter Luckett, Jr., said, "My family was always project oriented. We lived in them all—Father Panick, P. T., the Green Apartments. But I was not raised to be a gangster. I was taught that God put me down here for a purpose. I had good parents. Good parents make good kids. Bad parents teach kids to hate, they teach them fear and prejudice. I got guidance from my parents. My father was always on my back. He never let me rest. There were so many rules in our house! But I'm grateful for that. When I went out I had to be home by midnight. When the party got jammin' I had to get goin'.

"My mother was a very clean person. She always had food on the table. She was always home. If my mother was not home when I got home from grammar school, I'd cry. I really appreciate that. I owe my parents a lot. It takes a lot for parents to raise four boys to love one another. I vowed I'd always be an example to the family for my parents' sake. They were good parents. They made a decision for me at an early age. They saw the change I needed so they got me into St. Augustine's.

"My family was different from most ghetto blacks. We always worked. The kids worked in the summer. It was the best of times. It got us through the winter. We had our own money so our parents didn't have to worry about us. Nobody gave us anything. Maybe other blacks resented us. It wasn't that we thought we were better than them, it was just that we were a close family. Other blacks never knew what we had, what our values were, but they were always scoping on us. You know, watching. And even more so when I got in the limelight. We had to uphold our image. We were the Lucketts! My father taught us a lot of pride. You ask anyone in the projects about the Lucketts!

"My father made us competitive among ourselves, too. He was always tellin' my brothers, 'Walter did this in Little League,' or 'Walter did that in Biddy Basketball.' Some people say my brothers were overshadowed by me, but that's only in those people's eyes. We're all leaders, not followers. It came from my father. He was a heavy dude, a helluva man. He was always there for us.

He coached Little League and Biddy Basketball and PONY baseball, just like a lot of white fathers. We were always playing on a team he coached. He loved to be around kids, white and black. He said he never was a kid. He went to work at twelve. Every job he ever had he became the boss, sometimes even over Ph.D's. Yeah, he's a heavy dude. But he drinks a lot. He regrets the things he missed and he takes it out on himself. My father can talk. *Talk!* He's a politician. A con man. He speaks seven languages. He'll brag on you till it embarrasses you. With me it's as if he's proving he's done something in life through me. That's why you have to put up with his garbage sometimes. I love him. He can't help it. But sometimes . . . like, one time, he got religion. He comes in the house his eyes rolling to heaven and his hands in prayer. 'I found the Lord, Butch,' he says. 'Salvation is mine!' For the next six days he don't drink, he don't cuss, he comes home right after work for supper. Then one night he comes in at midnight. He's holding his head and screaming, 'Shit, these goddamn kids, I'm gonna kill them! Make me a hamburger, woman!' Then the stupid nigger falls asleep in a chair. Next morning he says, 'Butch, I don't know what come over me. The devil got me, Butch.' I don't know, maybe he's goin' through a change or something. He's my father and I love him, but he's crazy. . . . I have to stay away from him. It hurts me. I stay away for a week and then he'll call and say, 'Butch,' —that's my nickname—he'll say, 'Butch, I got something I wanna talk to you about.' He don't really, but I go over anyway. We rap for a half-hour and then all that damn stuff starts all over again. He be drinking with his friends.

"His friends, now, that's a different story. He don't

have the best of friends. He's got some clowns. His friends don't do nothin'. They're what I don't ever want to be. Some of them are white guys. They're always in our house eating and drinking. Every one of them speaks a different language. Our neighbors are Puerto Rican. When their daughter was gonna have a baby, my father drove her and her nine relatives to the hospital in his little Vega. I get tired of that stuff, though. So many different types of people. Sometimes I just want to get away."

Sitting in George Fasolo's office in the Sheehan Center on that afternoon in 1967, Walter Luckett thought about the advantages his talent and his association with the Center had brought him and his family. They were many, and now, after his triumph in Ridgefield, there was another: the promise of a college education. Dr. Peter Yanity, the recruiter for Ohio University who had seen Walter play in Ridgefield, assured him he would get a scholarship to Ohio U. if his career continued to progress as it had so far. It would be a step out of the ghetto for Walter, a step out of Bridgeport into a life he had only begun to dream about with the advent of his associations with whites at the Sheehan Center. Understanding all these things, then, Walter swallowed his pride and apologized to Fasolo, then waited three hours to apologize to his teammates, then was told they had voted by the barest of margins to allow him to return to the team. He was thrilled they had, but stunned, too, by such a close vote in his favor. He was, of course, unaware that Fasolo had lied to him and that his teammates had voted unanimously to take him back. And he still did not grasp the magnitude of his transgression, did not see that it was a transgression at all. But he did not worry about it. He made his decision to apologize. He was simply exercising a virtue, humility, that had been preached to him by his godfather. It was not a virtue common to the ghetto, where pride held sway. There face, and the saving of it, was the primary virtue. Few ghetto blacks would have opted for Walter's choice, but such a decision came easy to him. In fact, it was not even a decision, really. Walter Luckett, Jr., was merely exercising a virtue that had already become part of his nature.

If Walter was aware of the benefits to be had from his association with the Sheehan Center, his father was even more so. He realized, for the first time, what his son's talent could do for him and his family—things that, it seemed, would never be within his power to achieve. George Fasolo says of Mr. Luckett, "After we got Walter into St. Augustine's and the family into the Green Apartments, Mr. Luckett realized he had a product in Walt. The whole family became users." Mr. Nocciolli echoed Fasolo's sentiments when he said, "Walt, Jr., saw whites who could afford to do things for him, and were willing to, and I'm afraid it affected him."

Don Clemmons, one of Walter Luckett, Jr.'s, closest black friends and also a close friend of Frank Oleynick and Barry McLeod, first met Walter and his father when both boys were stars in Little League. "I had heard of Walter Luckett but I'd never met him," says Clemmons, "until one day we were supposed to play against each other in a Little League game. Mr. Luckett calls my house and asks my father if he'd like to bet a little money on the game. Now, my father is a minister, and he didn't believe in no gambling, so he says, 'No thank you.' Then Walter gets on the phone and asks for me. He say, 'I'm

Walter Luckett. I hear you gonna pitch tomorrow. Well, so am I, and I'm gonna beat you.' I said, 'No, I don't think you will.' Then he says he wants to make a bet on the game, and I told him I can't do that, I'm the son of a preacher. Anyway, we end up bettin' a Coke. The next day he hits a home run off me, and all the while he's running the bases he be pointin' a finger at me, yellin', 'Don't throw that stuff no more.' He jumped three feet in the air and landed on home plate with both feet. The next time up he tripled, then he doubled, and finally when he hit a ball back to me, I ran it all the way over to first base I was so glad just to get him out. But he still lost the game, on an error. He cried. Then he had to buy me the Coke. His father didn't hardly want to talk to my father. They were both Little League coaches. But Mr. Luckett, he looked down on my father because he was a janitor. It's like Mr. Luckett thinks he's in the upper echelon or sumthin'. One day my father, who was a janitor at City Hall, met Mr. Luckett there. He went up to him and Mr. Luckett, you know, played him off. He was with some white men. My father never forgot that. He told me when Little League was over I was on my own, and that Walter's problem would always be that his father would never let him go off on his own."

Warren Blunt, who is Walter's oldest and closest black friend, met Walter under circumstances similar to those of Don Clemmons. "We started out being rivals in grammar school," says Blunt. "Walter averaged 24.9 points per game in basketball and I averaged 25. We didn't like each other. We both had egos. Sometimes egos are a terrible thing. Ego stunts you from growing. It don't allow knowledge to come through. Walt got his ego from his father. He's very egotistical. He got an identity problem. He could pass for white. He's inclined to be with the white man. He respects the white man and he don't respect the black man. He thinks the white man has the answer, the secret for being on top. Sometimes Walt's father comes off as being a white man. Walt's a lot like him. He plays better around the white man. He'll put out more to get respect from the white man.

"One day when we were kids playing at Ellsworth Park, I told him he plays harder around the white man than he do around the brothers. He didn't comment. But I know it's because he believes if the white man gives you respect then you know you're *bad*. And here he is puttin' out against these white boys who were nowhere as good as him. It was a kick for those white boys, playing against Walter Luckett. Walt loves being put on a pedestal by whites.

"Walt's always been more of a kid than most guys his age. At home, his parents serve him like a king. He gets that from his father, too. It's a very male chauvinist house. 'I'm the God here!' Mr. Luckett likes to say. I remember once, a visitor to their house said there were bats in the house. Mr. Luckett said, 'What you mean, *bats!* Ain't no *bats* in *my* house!' Soon as he said that this bat flies right by him. He jumped up and started swinging at it until he knocked it down. Then he picks it up and says, 'This little bitty thing ain't gonna run me outta my house.' And the bat up and bites him. 'This sonuvabitch is still alive!' he shouts, and throws it out the window. His family told him to go to the hospital to get a shot, but he said he didn't need one. Of course, the next morning, he was there real early for his shot. Like I said, Mr. Luckett got this big ego. I think it's partly because he comes from a low environment—the ghetto. He lives in the ghetto, but because of Walter he's a king. A king in the ghetto, know what I mean? We call it, 'Eatin' gravy in the ghetto.' It makes him more snobbish, you see, than if he was living in Fairfield. That's the way Walter is, too. Mr. Luckett passed it on to him. I hate to say that, Walter's my best friend, he's my man, I love him, but still, that's the truth."

Frank Oleynick, Sr., and his sister, Fran Oleynick McLeod, were two of eight children of a wild, beautiful, fiery-haired woman who had had two husbands, an Italian and a Slovak, and an even greater succession of boyfriends. Mary Langdon Oleynick Valentine could trace her ancestry back to Hungarian royalty and gypsies. Her mother had been a wealthy property owner in Hungary who, one day, was stricken with a mysterious illness that none of her doctors could diagnose. In desperation, her sister took her out into the country to a band of gypsies whom, she hoped, would cure her. Not only was she cured but she also fell madly in love with the gypsy leader. She stayed with him for a few days, then returned home to her husband. Nine months later she presented her husband with a baby girl they named Mary. Mary was different from her sedate, towheaded siblings. She had brilliant red hair and an equally fiery temperament. When her family went to chapel to say their rosaries, Mary, as a child, would go to the music room and pound wildly on the piano.

Life for Mary and her family changed drastically when the Russians confiscated her family's property after the turn of the century. By then, too, Mary was as wild as a gypsy, and so she was sent with an uncle to America. She eventually settled in Bridgeport, where she lived a precarious existence populated with a succession of boyfriends. Her life was finally stabilized for a time when she married John Oleynick, a sober, hard-working country boy from Czechoslovakia. When her husband died suddenly, Mary's life again took a turn for the worse. She lived, with her eight children, in increasingly poverty-stricken circumstances. At various times the state would take away her children for brief spells. A daughter Fran, who had osteomyelitis at an early age, was taken by the state so she could be given medical treatment she could not receive at home. Soon Mary's life was one of despair and she liked to say that she had been cursed by gypsies. "They cursed me and all my offspring," she would say dramatically.

When Frank Oleynick, Sr., was growing up in Bridgeport during the late 1930s he had little time for sports. Sports were a leisure activity, and young men like himself had no time for leisure. More often than not, boys had to go off to work before they reached their teens. It was not until after World War II, with the rise of affluent America, that youngsters, like his son, could afford to express their burgeoning manhood through sports. For those post-war youths, athletic performance would give them an identity which was a metaphor for manhood, something they would not actually acquire until somewhat later in life. Boys of Mr. Oleynick's day could not afford such luxuries. They did not need metaphors for manhood. They worked like men when only in their teens, and to express their manhood, they fought like men. As a young man, Mr. Oleynick's peers considered him one of the toughest in the city. His only rival as a street fighter was a skinny, light-skinned black named Walter Luckett. Each day to and from grammar school Luckett and Oleynick, then boys, would try to settle with their fists the issue of who was the best. The final tally of those many fights is still in doubt. Mr. Oleynick and his son claim he got the measure of Mr. Luckett, while Mr. Luckett and his son claim the opposite. Both fathers still admit that their encounters were brutal.

Beyond their mere prowess as fighters, Frank Oleynick, Sr., and Walter Luckett, Sr., had many things in common. Both came from large, very poor families. Both men quit school and went off to work at the age of twelve. Both men worked in a meat market. Both men also worked construction. And both men built reputations as drinkers. But here the similarities stop. Mr. Oleynick was a different kind of drinker than Mr. Luckett. He did not drink to clarify visions so much as to shroud realities. He drank to obliterate, not elucidate. Mr. Oleynick did not have many visions, nor did he have Mr. Luckett's ability to conjure them up. Mr. Oleynick saw mostly the past, not the future; he saw what had been, not what could be. And what he saw depressed him as he drank. Unlike Mr. Luckett, he did not grow garrulous and expansive. He hunched forward, curling his body around the bar in a fetal position. His face grew dark, and he glowered up through thick, black brows. With drink, Mr. Oleynick became hostile and his words, now sparsely given, had a cutting edge. He spoiled for a fight.

In his fifties now, Mr. Oleynick is a squat, barrel-chested man with unusually long arms. He walks hunched forward, his long arms dangling at his sides, the palms of his hands facing behind him. He has shining, swept-back black hair, dark eyes and an aquiline nose that, like the rest of his face, is blotchy. He was once extremely handsome. In his youth he was a ladies' man and was often in the company of beautiful women, although it seemed he would never take one seriously enough to get married. To him they were merely adornments. But women were greatly attracted to him. They admired his dark good looks, but even more his virile demeanor. He was a man's man, a tough, strong, even coarse man, whose very coarseness was alluring to women. He worked hard, played hard and drank hard. At the end of a day's work on construction, he would take off his shirt, throw it over his shoulder and walk to the nearest bar. Women were drawn, too, by his dark, threatening moods. He was alternately silent and volatile, given to mercurial changes of mood. He would show affection in a rough way, pinching a child's cheeks until they showed a bruise. Once, kissing his young niece, he bit her playfully until he drew blood. Says a relative of Mr. Oleynick's, "There was something about him. It would just come out. A mood would take over and what was just seconds before a rough but good-natured man became someone who, one felt, truly wanted to hurt you. He was a wild man at times. When he drank he got vicious. It seemed, at times, as if he was out to do as much damage in this world as possible."

Frank Oleynick, Sr., was twenty-four years old when his sister Fran introduced him to her best girl friend, Mary Ann Dwyer, a tall, attractive nurse who, like himself, had come from a large, poor, inner-city family. Mae, as she was called by her friends, was the most gregarious member of an essentially devout Irish Catholic family. She liked to have a good time. Often she could be seen at one of the city's many nightclubs with

Fran. And like her new boyfriend, she enjoyed taking a drink. Says a female relative of Frank's, "I don't think those two should ever have met. They might have saved themselves if they had married someone else. Mae was a tense, brittle girl, who seemed ready to crack from day one. But she really was a nice person. She always tried so hard to be affectionate that, at times, she was suffocating. She was a big, strong woman, and when she would hug the kids in our family she'd almost crush them.

"I always loved Frank, even more than my own father. When I was a little girl he would play games with me and take me everywhere with him. He'd sit me on his knee, hold me tight and call me 'Honey.' As I got older I could always tell him my problems and he'd listen. I didn't like Mae very much, although she was always nice to me. Maybe it was just female jealousy even then.

"I don't think Frank had any intention of marrying Mae at first. He dated her only as a lark. They both liked to have a good time. They were different kinds of drinkers, though. She got gregarious, and Frank, well, he was a shot-and-a-beer drinker.

"Anyway, like I said, Mae was always nice to me. I remember one time, I was thirteen I think, I was going to give a recital in school. My own parents didn't come, but Mae and Frank did. Mae helped paint my face. She also pinned up my hula skirt. I did a two-minute hula dance, and throughout the whole thing I remember hearing Frank and Mae applauding wildly and yelling, 'Bravo! Bravo! Bravo!' Just before I finished my dance my skirt slipped down around my knees. It seemed that when Mae had pinned it up she was already half in the bag. Anyway, without missing a beat I just wiggled low to the floor, slipped my skirt back up, then left the stage.

Afterwards, Frank told Mae I showed real class the way I didn't panic in front of all those people. 'This kid's so cool, honey!' he said. 'I can see her name in lights someday. M-U-D!' And then he laughed. He always liked me, he said, because I had balls. That was the way he talked, even to a young girl. More than anything, he admired guts.

"But no matter how much I appreciated that kind of thing from Frank, as I got older I began to realize he was a loser, at least as far as society saw him. He was okay as a construction laborer, but every time he tried to go into business he would fail. In his later years he worked for his older brother, John, who owned a market in downtown Bridgeport. Frank was the butcher. Eventually everyone in the family would work for John—Mae, Fran, even little Frankie. They all seemed to resent John, though. Frank liked to think that John exploited him just because Frank had to work for him. But it wasn't John's fault. He was a super guy. He was always bailing Frank out of his scrapes. He even set Frank up in another market, but before long Frank blew it and had to go back to work for John again. No, they resented John because he was so straight and successful and he had this dutiful Italian wife who worked by his side while the rest of them, well, they'd spend their time drinking. Frank would come home from the market in black moods. He wouldn't say anything. He'd just drink a lot of beer or whiskey and then, finally, blurt out his latest failure."

Frank Oleynick and Mae Dwyer were married six years before they had their first child, whom they named Frank, Jr. During those early years they lived in a number of homes scattered throughout the poorer sections of the city before they finally settled in a tiny Cape Cod on

Woodrow Avenue a few blocks below the Beardsley Terrace Apartments. "There was a kind of barrenness about it," says a relative. "They had all this blue overstuffed furniture and glass-mirrored tables. It reminded me of the kind of homes you find near the amusement park at Savin Rock." According to that relative, the Oleynick's life was as drab as the decor of their house. There were rumors of drinking bouts and marital discord that grew worse through the years. "To this day," says that relative, "I think they might have saved their marriage if Frankie, Jr., had come along earlier, but by the time he did, it was too late. At first Frank, Sr., had no interest in his son, but by the time Frankie was five he started to try to make a man of him. He'd call him over and Frankie, Jr., would start shaking like a leaf. He'd start whining, 'Mommy, Mommy.'

"I never really liked Frankie, Jr., when he was a kid. He was a sissy and, besides, he stole my thunder. Mae liked him more than me, naturally, and even Frank, Sr., split his affection between me and Frankie. I used to have to babysit for Frankie, and when no one was around I'd slap the shit out of him. One time, I remember, Mae and Frank were raising chickens for some extra money and I was sent out to the coop to candle and weigh the eggs. Frankie was with me. He was about seven, I think. I grabbed him by the neck and said, 'Listen, you little fuck, I don't wanna do this so you're gonna do it.' I taught him how to candle and weigh the eggs and then left him alone. I went into the house to do my hair and paint my nails and listen to rock music. Oh, I was a real princess in those days. Anyway, by the time I got back to the coop Frank had gone berserk. He had broken seventeen dozen eggs. He was standing in the middle of the coop, holding eggs up into the air, looking at them and then saying, 'Hmmm, medio,' and then he'd throw it against the wall, 'Splat.' Then he'd take another, 'Smalleo, splat,' and another, 'Largeo, splat.' The walls were all splattered with eggs. We both got the shit beat out of us for that. Another time, Frankie had this pet chick he said he loved. One day he squeezed its neck so hard its head popped off. He said he loved it. He thought he was showing it love, and I guess when you were raised like he was you begin to think that you show love through abuse."

Frank Oleynick, Jr.'s, childhood was somewhat more depressed than that of his cousin and close friend, Barry McLeod, who would one day star with him on the Notre Dame High School basketball team. Barry's mother, Fran Oleynick McLeod, married Ed McLeod, a former sailor and Bridgeport machinist, when she was twenty-three. She had her first son, Barry, six years later. Today, in his sixties, Ed McLeod is a mild-looking man, soft-spoken and reticent, who views the world through small, round eyeglasses. At one time he was legendary in Bridgeport as a beer drinker, but when doctors discovered he had an ulcer fifteen years ago, he was forced to stop drinking entirely. His life since then has been simple: work, television and the evening newspapers. In his later years, after his wife had died of cancer, Ed McLeod, wearing only underwear, would sit in silence for hours in the couple's small living room in their Cape Cod on Chamberlain Street, at the foothills of the Beardsley Terrace Apartments. He would become animated only when his son, Barry, now in his early twenties, came home late at night after having consumed large quantities of beer.

"Oh, Ed used to love his beer," said Barry recently. "Everyone in our family loved their beer. Frank's parents loved their booze, too. Now Ed gets his rocks off seeing me drunk. He'll say, 'What time did you come home last night, boy? Four A.M.? Oh, you're a drunken s.o.b.' And then he'll cackle to himself. He loves it. That's about all he says to me now, since my mother died. He's lost without her. He doesn't seem to be interested in anything. He cries all the time. He just sits there. You see what he's doing, watching TV and reading the papers, that's all he's ever done. He worked in Bridgeport Machines for thirty years. He never went on a vacation. My mother went alone. She went to Hawaii, she went to Las Vegas. He just sits there. It bothers me that people cut him up. It's not for me to say anything, I never lived with a woman for thirty-two years. But he never said much to me. We never had no father-and-son talks. If I had a problem I went to my mother. As far as my story's concerned, my father ain't no actor. He's just a spectator."

A relative of Barry McLeod says of his father, "Ed was a weak guy. Fran was the strength of that family. She liked to think of herself as the matriarch of the whole family. She was always telling everyone, including her brother Frank, what to do. She was a tough, bossy woman who was always much tougher on Barry than Mae was on Frankie. Barry wasn't like Frankie. He was more introverted and quiet. I guess you could say Barry's home life was a bit more stable than Frankie's, but there was still one thing both of those homes had in common —drinking.

"They'd all get so bad with their drinking I was afraid one day they'd hurt one of the kids. I remember one time, they were all drinking and Frank, Sr., went after Eddy. At the time Frankie and Barry were only little kids. They were playing together over in the corner of the room. They both looked up at what was happening and then, without even blinking, went back to playing. It was like nothing unusual was happening for them. I always thought that all the crazy things that had happened to Frankie and Barry would warp them. I think they did affect Frank more than they did Barry. Frank was very sensitive as a little kid, and yet there was a touch of cruelty about him. He said he loved those chickens, for instance, but one day I came home and found he had turned off the incubator and killed them all. . . . I don't know, our whole family seems to have suffered so much. There's all this terrible sadness in our lives. Maybe Frankie's grandmother Mary was right—there *is* a gypsy curse on us all."

four

Frank Oleynick, Jr., and Barry McLeod's earliest memories are of one another. They remember playing together in a sandbox; they remember sleeping together in the same bed. They remember the first time they ever shot a basketball at a basket. "I was a year younger than Barry," says Frank, "and a lot tinier. I held the ball behind my head with two hands and just threw it at the basket. It didn't reach. Barry says to me, 'You stink! Watch me. This is the way you're supposed to do it.' And he holds the ball down around his nuts somewhere and tries to shoot it and he don't even come close. I said to him, 'You stink, too.'"

Frank Oleynick and Barry McLeod remember such things because from their infancy they began to form a bond of friendship that would grow more and more solid through the years until, finally, it had become as strong as any relationship could possibly be. This closeness developed for a number of reasons, though it sprang from the fact that since both sets of parents spent so much time together, it was inevitable their sons would too.

Furthermore, because of their parents' excessive drinking, the boys were excluded from most conventional social relationships. Their parents did not associate with their neighbors, nor even, for that matter, with their own relatives who failed to share their common interest. Drinking united the Oleynick and McLeod families while isolating them from most other families. For instance, Frank, Jr., is bitter that his father's brother, John, excluded the Oleynick family from many of his own family's activities. "I always felt shitty toward my uncle," said Frank recently. "It's that old rich man, poor man story. My father was a fighter and my uncle was a businessman. His wife pushed him to make money, and now he does everything with her family." This social ostracism embarrassed his father, claims Frank, Jr., and certainly, in turn, must have been an embarrassment for him.

From an early age Frank and Barry felt set apart from their own relatives, and so it was only natural that they would also feel set apart from society. This was another reason they turned to each other for companionship. It also made their parents' "differentness" strikingly apparent to them, and to varying degrees this became a source of discomfort. Out of loyalty they tried to protect their parents. Neither brought many friends to their homes, but those they did bring were almost always youths from similar backgrounds.

"Frank came to my house more times than I went to his," said Barry recently. "My house was always open to my friends. My mother would go out and come back with cases of beer for my friends." Since his parents' drinking was more excessive than his cousin's, Frank tried to protect his parents from scrutiny by not inviting many of his friends over to his house.

"Frank didn't like his mother and father much," says Walter Luckett, Jr. "They got on his nerves a lot.

Blacks accepted Frank before whites did. Frank got embarrassed when we came over and his mother was drinking. We'd have to go to his room. His parents were in another world. People didn't give them too much respect. Now that Frank's older, he cleaned up their name. He put a little class to them. I respect him for that."

Another friend of Frank's, Ron DelBianco, remembers the time he went to a Cub Scout meeting at the Oleynick home. "Frank's mother was high," says DelBianco, "and it embarrassed him." His high school basketball coach, John Waldeyer, says of Frank Oleynick's home life, "Socially and economically, his family was depressed. I was in his house only twice in four years. Whenever I would pick him up for a game or take him to school, he'd make a point of waiting for me at the front door."

Frank and Barry grew close too, out of necessity. They were whites in a predominantly black neighborhood. Not only did they have a skin color different from most of their peers, but they were also slightly better off. Also, because they lived in a tough neighborhood, they had to join forces simply to survive. Frank says, "Me, Barry and his brother Ron always stuck together. Anyone who beat up one of us knew he'd have to fight all three. Right or wrong, we stuck together. Guys would see Ron alone and they'd think of hittin' on him, but most of the time they'd think again because they knew sooner or later they'd have to mess with all three of us."

Frank and Barry also turned to one another for their amusements since their parents did not take a very active interest in their lives. A former football coach at Notre Dame High School says, "I used to drive by their house and see Frank and his sisters and Barry sitting on the curb. They played in the streets. It was dangerous. I don't think they ever had much parental supervision."

Frank and Barry were not the only youths in the Terrace area who were brought up this way. There were many others and most of them were black. "Frank and Barry grew up more like black kids than most black kids did," says Don Clemmons, a black friend. "In fact, their upbringing was more black than Walter Luckett's." Frank and Barry felt more secure with blacks than with many whites from a more conventional background.

In general, Frank Oleynick and Barry McLeod were raised in a peer-oriented society not unlike that of the youths in the novel *The Lord of the Flies*. Their upbringing, for all intents and purposes, was devoid of adults. They turned to themselves and their friends for amusements and even safety. Their own friendship and, later on, their friendship with other youths, mostly black, would become the focal point of their lives. They learned earlier than most to fend for themselves. They became, in short, parents to themselves and each other. "Frank was an old man very young," says a friend.

In time Frank Oleynick would become a parent to his younger sister. He would say, at the age of twenty, "When I was younger I had no influence over my older sister, even though she was two years younger than me. Now she seems like four years older. She got away from me. She was exposed to too much too fast. There was nobody there for her. Now my younger sister, she's only sixteen, there's still hope for her. She's gonna be a superstar someday. She's my heart, man."

"It's funny," says Walter Luckett, "but Frank always dated black girls, and yet he didn't want no brothers messing with his sisters. The older one was with brothers all the time. He didn't like it. Them brothers be swarming around like bees. But he didn't like that. One time I stopped by the market when he was there and I asked about his older sister. He gets real serious and says, 'Now, I don't want none of that shit, Walter.'"

Eventually, too, Frank Oleynick would become a parent to his parents. "I started worrying about my parents when I was in high school," he said in an interview when he was twenty years old. "I'm not in charge yet, but I can see it coming. I was on my own mentally at fifteen. I decided then what was best for me and did it, even if my father didn't understand it. Sometimes I tried to explain things to my father if I thought he could understand. For instance, my father never liked my associations with blacks. He worried I might get hurt, for one thing, and for another, he hated blacks. He had worked at the Mohican Market in downtown Bridgeport for so long that the only blacks he ever saw were prostitutes and junkies. He held that against all blacks. When I started dating, I never brought any black girls home to my house. He'd never accept my dating blacks. I never brought any girls home, for that matter. It was as simple as that. It wasn't like my father thought I was queer or anything. He knew I was dating. It was just that my parents were not the 'bring your girl home to dinner' kind.

"At first I tried to explain to my parents that my black friends were different. I explained that blacks were the best basketball players in the city and that I had made a decision to devote myself to basketball. My parents could not comprehend what was in my mind. At fifteen I had the faith I could do it. I understood myself better than my parents did. But finally I realized there was no way they'd ever understand my friendships with blacks or my devotion to basketball. I came to grips with that early. My father, he was hurt I didn't want to go work at the Mohican Market with him. He wanted me to be a butcher. I hated it. He called me a lazy bastard. I told him I could get a college scholarship through basketball. He laughed. He never believed it. He never saw any possibilities in sport. My father was not all that involved in my career when I was younger. He didn't go to my games in high school until my senior year when I was a star. A little star. He never lived his life through me. Now he knows all my statistics. He can tell you everything. I don't like to look at that as if it's bandwagon stuff. It's just, like I said, he never saw any possibilities in sport.

"My father never understood sports. He never was a kid. He had it rough. He started working at twelve. He got a banana for Christmas. He always had to work hard just to put food on the table for us. When I was in grammar school—it was mostly black—I started to stay out late. I was always getting into fights. He saw that, so he worked his ass off to send me to Notre Dame High School. You see, I didn't have such a bad childhood. Oh, I got my ass kicked quite a few times by my father, but we were not as poor as blacks. The only time I thought I missed something was when I was ten and I saw other fathers playing catch with their sons. But my father wasn't athletic. He never got into sports as a kid. He never was a kid. Now that he's older he likes to drink beer with my friends. He goes out drinking with Barry a lot. They're a lot alike. Now my father's like a kid."

Frank Oleynick and Barry McLeod were also drawn to one another because their personalities were compatible. Both were tough inner-city youths. Frank, although younger than Barry, was an extrovert and an egotist. He had a kind of belligerent independence not unlike his father's, bordering at times on contrariness. He seemed to assume stances merely for their shock value. Barry, on the other hand, was almost an introvert. He hovered in Frank's shadow, seldom speaking, and then only to deliver an exhortation or a phrase, rarely a sentence. And yet he was independent, although his independence was less visible than his cousin's, whom he often elected to follow. Barry's independence, unlike Frank's, seldom took the form of mere contrariness. "They both had those big egos," says Ron DelBianco. "They would walk into a McDonald's hamburger restaurant one at a time and then go and sit at different tables. They'd eat alone, as if they didn't want to be part of one another, then they'd get up and leave. First one, then the other. Even though they always hung together they had these big egos they had to maintain."

If Frank was a bit more intelligent than Barry (and coldly so), then Barry was more sensitive than Frank. When Frank erred it was generally on the side of coldness. Barry leaned toward sentimentality.

The first organized sports team that Frank Oleynick ever tried out for was his neighborhood Little League team. At the time he was seven, smaller and a year younger than his peers who were in the same grade in grammar school. (He would eventually graduate from high school before his seventeenth birthday.) "They wouldn't let me play because I was too young," he says. "I cried my ass off. So they made me a bat boy. Most of the players on my team were black. That was how my associations with them began. It was just a natural thing.

They were the people I played sports with. At first I never thought about them being black, and by the time I did, it was too late. My friendships with them had already been formed. Like I say, my associations were never a black-white thing, it was a friendship thing. For example, today I'm completely at home in the Terrace, which is all black, but I'd never think of going alone to Father Panik Village. I remember once when we were kids we had a game against the Panik. When we got there, they all had razor blades in their socks. Willie Murphy, one of our players, says, 'What the fuck is this, brothers? How you gonna play basketball with razor blades?'

"When I turned eight or nine, the trend in my neighborhood went from baseball, which was a white sport, to basketball. I just followed the trend. At the time I lived on Woodrow Avenue, one block up from Pitt Street near the Terrace. I had my own basket on a telephone pole and my own ball, but they wouldn't let me play. They called me the 'midget' and made me sit and watch them play with my ball and my basket. I'd sit on the curb and try to pick things up in my head. When the players left I'd practice what I'd seen them do."

Don Clemmons says of the young Oleynick, "Frank was different from most players, guys like Walter Luckett. They were physically talented at an early age and their talent carried them at first. Frank learned to play the game in his head first. A mental game."

Because Frank Oleynick learned to play basketball first in his head, it took him longer than most to become proficient at the game. However, once he grasped certain moves and principles, they became ingrained more firmly than in his more talented counterparts, who never had to think about why and how they did something on the court. For example, most younger players develop a jump shot according to "feel," learning to shoot the ball the way it seems most comfortable to them. When they lose that feel, it is very difficult for them to recapture it because they never understood the mechanics in the first place. Frank Oleynick studied his contemporaries, the way they spread their fingers across the ball and how they flicked it off their fingertips with a snap of their wrist, until he mentally and later physically mastered that "feel" in a way he would never forget.

All the players Frank watched and studied were black. This was to his benefit because, at the time, they were the best players around. Gene Mack was a textbook jump shooter, and so was Reggie Walker. "I used to dribble to Reggie's house and wake him up in the morning to come out and teach me to shoot," says Frank. "Oh, I was a real pain in the ass. Then there was Ronnie Pettaway, one of the best in the city. But he got into drugs and died in an automobile accident."

"Ronnie Pettaway's the one who taught me how to play," says Barry McLeod. "And when he got strung out there was nothing I could do to help him."

"It's funny," says Frank, "there were so many names, so many great players, guys who should have been but never were. They were my idols. Now they're nothing. But the greatest I ever saw was Sonny James. He was a legend in his own time."

Sonny James (not his real name) is now twenty-six years old. He has a cherubic face, glassy liquid-brown eyes, smooth shining skin, pouty lips and a voice that has all the soft hesitant sweetness of the absolutely self-assured. When Sonny speaks, his hands, palms out, massage the air in tender circles. He stands about six feet tall and moves with a languid grace. He is an immaculate dresser—pressed patchwork jeans, waist-length leather jacket, polished boots—in the fashion of most professional athletes, which he is not. Sonny is a criminal, and he is presently serving a twenty-year term for armed bank robbery. Within a period of six months, he robbed the same bank twice. The first time he wore jeans and a New York Knicks T-shirt and carried a small gym bag inside of which was sequestered a sawed-off shotgun. A few months later he entered that same bank wearing a maxicoat, a floppy hat and a full-faced beard, all of which gave him a striking resemblance to former New York Knicks' guard Walt "Clyde" (after Bonnie and Clyde) Frazier. He carried the sawed-off shotgun underneath his maxicoat. After the robbery he went to the Terrace where he showed one of his friends a paper bag with thousands of dollars in it.

"It was more money than I ever seen at one time in my life," says that friend. "I had to count it. I didn't think it was real. Sonny said, 'You want some too, come on with me.' I told him I was scared and I didn't want no part of that money. I knew Sonny. When we was kids we used to go to the Middle Street Boys' Club early in the morning and sleep inside it overnight."

"Sonny, he's a down dude," says another friend, Walter Luckett. "He's got style. He's an actor, man. I mean, he robbed this bank wearing a Clyde brim. He's an actor. I love Sonny. Everybody loves Sonny. He's a legend. But there's trouble in his blood. He's been in reformatories since he was eleven years old. At one time his father, his grandfather and he were all in the same joint. He's done everything. He's used to jail. It's his way of life. He robs a bank, lives good for a while, gets caught and does his time."

When Sonny James should have been graduating with his high school senior class, he was already serving a prison term for drug-related offenses. But when he was a high school sophomore, at the age of seventeen, he was an All-State guard on his high school basketball team and one of the smoothest backcourt players in the country.

"I compare Sonny to Earl Monroe," says Luckett. "He comes out with a bag of tricks. His shit is phenomenal. He should be paid for it. He shakes and bakes and spins and drops his J's like nobody I ever seen. Even on the court he was different."

"Sonny was ahead of his time," says Frank Oleynick. "He invented the spin move in Bridgeport when he was only fifteen. He'd go dribbling up to your face and then peel off your hip, turning his back on you while carrying the ball at his hip. The first time he did that on Pitt Street we started yelling, 'Sonny, you can't do that! That's carrying the ball! You'll never get away with that in organized ball.' He said, 'You watch me.' And sure enough, about then, who comes along but Clyde Frazier, and he gets away with it all the time now. But Sonny was the first player I ever saw make the spin move. He used to leave Don Clemmons on the floor. He used to make Walter Luckett cry, man. Even then Walter was great, but Sonny would steal his game and all the while be telling Walter what he was gonna steal from him. He'd say, 'Luckett, you ain't shit. I'm gonna block your shot.' And he would. Oh, man, he'd make Walter cry.

"Like I said, Sonny's game was ahead of its time," Frank reminisced." He had finesse. He had the pro touch the way he did things. Even when he fucked up, he fucked up in bigger and better ways than anyone I ever saw. But I learned from him. I used to sit on the curb and watch him. I learned to feel the texture of the ball. I learned to try to get dexterity in my fingertips. When Sonny would leave after a game on Pitt Street, I'd practice what I'd seen him do a million times. I always loved Sonny and he always liked Barry and me. Whenever he used to steal shirts, forty-dollar shirts, he'd always steal three and give one each to me and Barry. At the time, Sonny was a few years older than us and we really admired him. We loved him. We didn't realize then how bad things were. They say, in his sophomore year, Sonny turned almost his entire high school team on to drugs.

"I was one of the few white guys in the city to be influenced by black players like Sonny. Most of the white players were influenced by a player at Fairfield Prep named Jim Fitzsimmons, who went on to Duke and then transferred to Harvard. He was a suburban player with straight moves and a good long jump shot. He played more like Walt Luckett. Walt was more influenced by Fitzsimmons than I was, although I don't think Walt's strictly a suburban player. I first started hearing about Walt when I was almost nine years old. We've known about each other ever since, although even then I wasn't in his league. I was a marginal player and he was always a helluva player."

While still in grammar school, Barry and Frank were invited by their black friends to come up to the Terrace to play basketball in the outdoor Urban Coalition League. They were the only two white players to play in that league up to that time. "In any of the apartment buildings in the Terrace," says Barry McLeod, "there's only one thing you can smell. Urine. There's writing on all the walls and the doors. The pipes leak. The elevators never work. We were in an elevator one night going up to Kenny Sumpter's apartment when we noticed some brown stains on the floor. It was blood. The night before a girl had got shot in that elevator. The windows are mostly broke. There are gangs roaming through the halls. But we were never scared. We never got into a fight in the Terrace. It was growing up cool. Everything about the Terrace was cool then. Now, I see it's not so cool for the people who live there. It's fucked up. They got no hope."

"The Terrace was my home as a kid," says Frank Oleynick. "I was there every day."

"I was always a little apart from the Terrace," says Barry. "I never needed it. I had my family. I didn't need to look for people to understand me. But I guess Frank and I did use the Terrace as an escape. We used to climb out our windows at night and sneak up to the Terrace. Our parents couldn't believe we were just playing basketball until one o'clock in the morning. They worried about us getting hurt, maybe killed, or hooked on drugs. My mother used to say, 'Barry, ain't you got no white friends?'"

Frank Oleynick, Sr., was particularly volatile about his son's association with blacks. He says, "I didn't like it one bit. I had to learn to like it. I'd dealt with blacks at the market and, in their own words, they were 'motherfuckers.' Their pet word. I got to feel hatred for them. I took it out on all of them. But the kids Frankie grew up with were good. They respected my wife and daughters. What are you gonna do? It's a changing world. You got to adjust. I know one thing, Frankie wouldn'ta been no good in basketball without blacks."

"Our associations with blacks got us out of trouble more often than into trouble," says Frank, Jr. "One time me, Barry and his brother Ron beat up this white dude, and the next day a bunch of white kids came looking for us. David Lee, one of our black friends, was going to a party, and when he saw us in trouble he ran and got some of his friends to scare off those white kids. Another time this white kid got shot in a grammar school yard and the next day when we were walking through there these black dudes came after us. Again David Lee came by, and he told those brothers to leave us alone, we were cool.

"When we first went to the Terrace we had to prove ourselves. I developed a black style of play. I never consciously tried to emulate black players, it was just that I practiced the moves I saw everyone else doing and everyone else was black."

Frank Oleynick did not arbitrarily adopt all that he saw in the Terrace. He tempered the flamboyant, dribbling-behind-the-back black game with his own discipline and intelligence. He took the best from the Terrace, discarded the excessive, unnecessary flash and molded his own game of controlled flamboyance. "I didn't just play on instinct," he says. "I was always thinking a lot. I never did nothing for effect. I was conscious of body control and fundamentals, and I practiced over and over by myself. I played a mental game. I never went behind my back unless there was no other way to get by my man."

When Frank and Barry were about eleven they also began going to downtown Bridgeport to play basketball at the Middle Street Boys' Club. In their early teens they played on the Middle Street state team, whose arch rival was the Sheehan Center Trojans with star Walter Luckett. This was the first time Frank and Barry had an organized confrontation with Luckett, who invariably overshadowed them. While Frank and Barry struggled to score double figures, Walter seemed effortlessly to be able to drop thirty points a game. "Walt was always a star at the Sheehan Center," says Frank. "I couldn't afford to go there. Besides, it was too organized for its area. You had to have shorts and sneaks, and the only games they played were organized games. They organized kids right out of the Sheehan Center. At Middle Street there was always a pickup game going on, even if you did have to kick the rats out of the shower. Middle Street was a street thing. The best players in the city, except for Walt, went to Middle Street. This was to my benefit. I was playing against the best while Walt was a star against easy competition. Walt had early success, and people started grabbing hold of him to go up with him. Eventually they pulled him down. I was never in the limelight at that age so I was left alone to develop on my own."

There were many other talented youths at the Middle Street Boys' Club who were also left alone to develop on their own. But unlike Frank Oleynick, they did not have the discipline, diligence or intelligence to pick and choose properly from all that they saw at Middle Street. It was this ability of Oleynick's, his discriminating powers and his drive, that helped him develop his talent beyond that of his contemporaries.

"Walt's problem," says Barry, "was that his career was planned out for him step by step all his life. He had three coaches at the Sheehan Center and we were lucky to find one. Still, Middle Street was the best thing for us at the time. When they finally closed it down in our junior year of high school, we all cried."

One of Frank and Barry's teammates at Middle Street, and one of the only other whites to play there regularly, was Ron DelBianco. He remembers Frank and Barry less for their basketball talent than for their toughness. "Frank was the toughest kid I ever saw," says DelBianco. "He didn't walk, he swaggered, as if everybody should follow him. And they did. He had this charisma, an air about him. He always had groupies around him when he went on to high school. When he shaved his head one year, everybody did. When he bought a long coat with a fur collar, like a fag would wear, you would soon see six guys wearing the same. But this wasn't just an act. He really was one of the toughest guys I ever saw. I remember once when we were playing a pickup game at Middle Street and Frank kept beating this older black dude. This dude was getting frustrated, so one time he just ran right over Frank. Frank gets up and points a finger at him and says, 'Don't you ever do that again.' The black dude says, 'What you gonna do about it, white boy?' Frank hit him seven times before he could hit Frank once. Barry and I were the only other white guys there, and I was terrified. Barry faced off all the other blacks in the gym by himself. He says, 'Now don't you mess in this thing, brothers,' and believe it or not nobody interfered. I'm not sure if it was because they were all afraid of Frank and Barry or whether they just respected them so much they left them alone. Anyway, after the fight the guy who ran the club came over to Frank and said, 'I don't ever want to see you in here again, understand?' Frank points a finger at him and says, 'I'll be back tomorrow,' and he was.

"I remember another time when we were all playing Pop Warner football against a team from Fairfield that had one of the best halfbacks in the country. Frank was a linebacker, and he made a point of following this guy everywhere and hitting him whether he had the ball or not. Every time he'd knock this kid down, he'd stand over him and point at him and say, 'You're a no-good motherfucker.' Frank was only thirteen at the time. The kid was terrified of Frank by the end of the game. When he finally did manage to score a touchdown with Frank chasing him, the kid turned around in the end zone and sees Frank still coming after him. The kid kept on running right out of the end zone with Frank still chasing him. Frank was merciless."

By the time Barry McLeod and Frank Oleynick were sophomores at Notre Dame High School they were still not accepted by, nor had they accepted, their school's white student body. Most of their classmates, like themselves, were lower-middle-class ethnics, but few had been raised so close to a large black ghetto. Frank and Barry had wanted to go to Central High School, an inner-city, predominantly black school noted for its great basketball teams, but their parents insisted on their going to Notre Dame. Most of their black friends had gone to Central.

At Notre Dame Barry and Frank felt they did not fit, which was accurate for a number of reasons, all stemming from their peculiar upbringing. They talked black. They called one another "bro," short for brother, and tossed around expletives such as "motherfucker" with the abandon none of their white contemporaries could ever muster. They dressed black—high-cut colored sneaks and dress pants and silky shirts and even big, floppy, peaked caps called "the big apple." And they acted black. They were constantly slapping each other's palms and strutting and swaggering through the corridors with a cool belligerence and street-smart cynicism that seemed beyond their age, prompting their fellow students to see them as affected. Furthermore, their close association with Notre Dame's few black students, such as Donald Clemmons, confused the rest and frequently brought Frank and Barry to the point of fisticuffs. Once in the cafeteria some white students called Clemmons a bear and started pitching pennies at him. Frank, Barry and his brother Ron sprang to Clemmons' defense, and a fight ensued. Thereafter the three white youths were known as "nigger lovers," an appellation enhanced by their appreciation of such black musicians as the Jackson Five rather than the more conventional white groups of the time like Crosby, Stills, Nash, and Young.

Bruce Webster, a local college coach who was beginning to take an interest in Frank and Barry, noted their difficulty in adjusting to Notre Dame: "Their black thing was a necessity for them. They couldn't have white friends. They were poor, they came from a black environment and they weren't that easy to like. They were both moody and had a chip on their shoulders. They didn't do things white kids did. They didn't have a car or any interest in driving one. They didn't date girls or go to dances either. All they did was play basketball twenty-four hours a day, and not many whites wanted to do that. Only the blacks did, and so they were the only ones left to turn to."

John Waldeyer, their high school coach, adds, "Frank did not have a driver's license until he was twenty because he had no interest in driving. His attitude was, it's hard to play basketball in a car. I think Frank emulated blacks simply because they were the best basketball players and he was dedicated to basketball. If the best basketball players had been Irish, Frank would have been speaking with a brogue. Frank's the kind who, if he does something, does it all the way. He *had* to go out with black girls. He had to wear those big apple caps and act cool and say 'man' all the time. Frank is a single-minded person. He's fanatic about basketball. It's something he learned early he could do well, and that's all he ever wanted to do. He resented other people who didn't have his interest in basketball. He would dribble a basketball to school in the snow. He was fanatical. Barry was just dedicated to basketball. He was nicer than Frank, but Frank had the charm when he wanted to use it."

Whites, like Waldeyer, claim that Frank and Barry deliberately excluded themselves from their school's social life. "Whites wanted to like them," says Waldeyer, "but they just made it hard to." Frank and Barry claim the opposite. "From the first, we were outcasts," says Barry. "We never went to a social event. I hated Notre Dame."

At times it did seem that Frank and Barry had nothing in common with their fellow white students. Studies meant nothing to them. They had no desire, common to the children of ethnics, to improve their social lot over that of their parents through the conventional means of education. They often cut classes to listen to music in the locker room or, on days they had no basketball game, they simply failed to go to school at all.

"Waldeyer would come looking for us," says Frank.

"We'd be playing basketball at some grammar school court, and he'd drive up and motion us over to his big Caddy. We wouldn't go. We ignored him."

In school Frank and Barry were troublemakers. Beyond their belligerent attitudes, they would often turn an attempt by students, faculty or administration to make their stay at Notre Dame more palatable into an opportunity to cause trouble. They were made school janitors, for example, a job that required little real effort but would help defray the costs of their tuition, which their parents had trouble meeting. They repaid that consideration one day by blowing up the chemistry laboratory. "There was mercury balls all over the place," says Barry. "Frank stole some syringes for a junkie friend. The school attached three of our pay checks for the damage."

Their first two years at Notre Dame were further complicated by the fact that neither of them had yet exhibited the kind of basketball talent that would bloom suddenly in their junior year and would pave their way more easily into the mainstream of the student body.

"As freshmen they were nothing, and as sophomores they were only a little better," says Dave Bike, their junior varsity coach and a man who would have a great influence over Frank Oleynick's career and his life. Bike, a former Notre Dame High School basketball and baseball star, is a big, gentle man who bears a striking resemblance to Pete Rose. However, he had none of Rose's single-minded aggressiveness as an athlete. Whereas Rose is the kind of man who says, "I live for 200 hits a year," Bike, in a short minor league baseball career, could never seem to muster such cockiness. He says of one of his minor league seasons, "I was hitting

.360 at Montgomery, Alabama, by midseason and I said to myself, 'Hell, I'm not this good,' and sure enough I ended the season at .260."

"My peers were better players than me," says Frank Oleynick. "Barry and Dennis McLaughlin made the junior varsity when they were freshmen. I played on the freshman team. And Walter Luckett, hell, he was a star on the Kolbe varsity when he was a freshman. He was so far above me that a comparison was not even drawn then. But it didn't matter, because ever since my freshman year I was determined to be the best."

By the end of their sophomore year, Frank and Barry began to show flashes of the kind of talent that would soon blossom, yet they still acted as if they were outsiders, even among their own teammates. Says Dave Bike, "Frank was always moody. He was cocky. He never backed down from a fight. He always acted as if he should run the whole show. When one of his teammates messed up on the court, Frank would embarrass him. I think it all sprang from his background. He was defensive about it. I always thought Frank and Barry were lacking something. Frank would play this role, and when he got trapped or embarrassed he would get aggressive. Barry was quieter. He would put his chin down. He was never aggressive when trapped. He would withdraw."

Because Frank and Barry posed such problems, and because he thought they might be able to help his varsity team as juniors, head coach John Waldeyer called on a friend, Bruce Webster, the basketball coach at the University of Bridgeport, to help him out. Waldeyer felt that Webster, a tough New Jersey kid in his youth, might be able to communicate more easily with his two players.

Waldeyer, from a white suburban background, a German scholar and a gourmet cook, had little in common with the two. Waldeyer also hoped Webster would communicate to Frank and Barry the possibility that they might be able to use their basketball talent to go on to college when they graduated from Notre Dame.

"John Waldeyer told me they had no direction at home," says Webster, a pale, soft-looking, blond-haired man in his early forties. "In all the years I knew them I never met Frank's father until Frank was in his twenties. He never mentioned his family. As sophomores in high school they were difficult. They were nonverbal, except with their friends. They only talked basketball. Frank had a chip on his shoulder and Barry was suspicious. They just turned off of people. If you hit them between the eyes with something they didn't like, they'd just turn you off. At the time I was going to have a summer basketball camp for area high school players, and so I invited Frank and Barry and told them they didn't have to pay. But I told them they would have to help me out at the camp to earn their keep. I also made them pay off the camp by working around my house. They'd move furniture or go to the dump with me. Sometimes I'd hand them a $10 bill. I tried to help them slowly, but not forcefully. They started to kid me and say I was commercializing them, you know, making money off them. Frank said to me, 'Someday I won't ever have to do this shit.'

"I was always closer to Frank than to Barry. Frank was more receptive. He asked me questions and sought advice. Barry was softer and quieter. He would never express displeasure at anything. You never knew with him. After awhile they started to play one-on-one against me in my backyard. Their whole ambition was to beat me, and they couldn't. But it was the beginning of a bond of friendship between us. The only time we would argue was over different players they admired. They loved John Williamson, who then played on a high school team in New Haven and went on to stardom with the New York Nets. I told them he was a selfish player. They couldn't see that. They only admired the end result. It's funny, I got along with Frank and Barry but I have a reputation among blacks in this area as being antiblack. I don't have them on my team. They're trouble. I knew if I ever got Frank and Barry at the University of Bridgeport they'd be trouble, too. But I figured I could handle them."

By their junior years at Notre Dame, Frank and Barry were averaging well into double figures per game, and with their success came acceptance from the school's whites, an acceptance they both resented. Barry says, "I didn't like the idea that nobody accepted us until we got good in basketball. They used to laugh at the way we talked. They mocked us. They thought we were putting on." Then gradually throughout the year, their attitudes softened and they moved into the mainstream of the student body. Frank was a charismatic figure at the school. He had a legion of "groupies," youths who had once ridiculed his style and now tried their best to emulate it. Even Barry, normally taciturn, had his fans. "This one kid loved Barry so much," says Frank, "that Barry charged him a dime just to hang with him. Then one day in the cafeteria he says, 'Heh, listen Grub, next week it's gonna cost you a quarter.'" It was also about this time that Frank and Barry became conscious of the rewards basketball might bring them. Now success brought them acceptance, but in the future it might produce more tangible rewards.

Frank and Barry achieved their modest success as juniors and their more flamboyant success as seniors through hard work. Barry, the more talented of the two, was a dedicated player. Frank, slower and less physically talented, was fanatical about his sport. Donald Clemmons remembers, "Frank Oleynick's determination was the biggest thing. If he had a bad game he'd work harder to correct his mistakes. He had that kind of mental discipline. One morning I went to work out with him. He ran two miles at the beach and then ran up and down the steps at old Central High School fifteen times. Then he went out to Lake Mohegan and, while everyone else was looking at the girls, Frank swam back and forth across the lake. All the girls were going, 'Oh, Frankie! Oh, Frankie!' but he didn't know nothin'. I said to myself, this cat crazy. Then he goes up to Trumbull to an outdoor court and plays twelve or thirteen hard games, and still he ain't eat yet. Finally he gets a quart of orange juice and a hamburger, and I say, 'Drop me off home, I'm done.' He say, 'No! I ain't finished yet. I got to go back to Lake Mohegan.' Now the lake is closed, there's no lifeguard and it's dark, but still he starts swimming from one end to the other. That was the kind of workout he did every day. I'd be at his house and I'd have to sit and watch while he did 1000 sit-ups."

John Waldeyer says that in addition to Frank's mental discipline, his greatest asset was his ability to know how to practice alone. "He'd dribble two balls the length of the court, then go back and do spin dribbles. He had a whole routine before our practices. He'd practice passing against the walls. He'd dribble between chairs. He'd do all this for one hour before he ever took a shot at the basket. Like I said, Barry was dedicated but Frank was fanatical. Barry looked at life as being more than basketball. I always wondered, with Frank, what he'd do when his legs didn't work."

"I always thought Barry was better than Frank," says Dave Bike. "But Frank was a year younger and two years younger than Luckett, and I guess it just took him longer to catch up to them. He had to extend himself more than the others. Anytime Frank played a good game, I knew he'd been practicing a lot in the gym. The kind of things he was doing, dribbling behind his back and all, had to be perfectly timed."

Frank Oleynick's game looked "natural" to the uninitiated, but it was not. From the stands the average fan never saw that his flamboyant moves were all a bit stylized. They had the look of something learned, not instinctive. Ron DelBianco, who often played against Frank and Barry earlier, says, "I always thought Barry was a better player than Frank because he had no pattern. Frank had a series of moves, almost a routine, that looked instinctive at first but were really just part of a whole pattern he'd devised in the gym." As proof of Oleynick's routine, DelBianco pointed out that at times when Frank went into his left-right-left-right Earl Monroe move, he seemed to lose sight of his defensive man because he was so intent on his moves. Often, he would fake out his man on one move and then, not conscious that he had been successful, would continue, which allowed the defensive man time to regroup. In short, he often made one too many a fake.

The summer after his junior year, Frank Oleynick left Bridgeport and his cousin Barry McLeod for the first time in his life. He traveled with Bruce Webster to Sydney, New York, north of Binghamton, to participate in the Golden Valley Basketball Camp. The camp was composed of high school students, most of whom were classic white suburban players. "I didn't want to go," says Barry. "I knew there'd be no competition." Frank was the immediate hit of the camp. "He averaged about fifty points a game," says Webster. "He's still a legend there. The fans and players never saw anything like him. The millionaire owner of the camp loved Frank. He bought him a new pair of sneakers. 'You're the greatest,' he told Frank. And then, to anyone who would listen, he'd say, 'Do you believe it?' That was the first time Frank was ever away from Barry, and yet he had a great time. He loved the country living. Everyone there studied Frank. He had this charisma. I think it was there, for the first time in his life, that it dawned on Frank what his talent could do for him. I think, too, he realized for the first time that he might someday be in Walter Luckett's league as a basketball player."

Their senior year at Notre Dame Frank and Barry blossomed as basketball players. They each averaged well over twenty points a game, and they led their team to the city championship with two victories over Walter Luckett's Kolbe team. Frank and Barry had some beautiful games. Against Stratford High they missed a total of two shots, with Barry scoring thirty-six points and Frank thirty-four. They both were named to the All-State team and were feted at a *New York Daily News* luncheon in New York City. Returning from that luncheon with Coach John Waldeyer and some black players from surrounding towns, Sammy Miller, a cousin of the professional Calvin Murphy, said to Frank, "Why do you talk the way you do? You ain't black." Frank was embarrassed and fell silent.

Notre Dame, behind Frank and Barry, also beat perennially powerful Central High. The Central team was all black, and in the jubilant Notre Dame locker room after the game, Frank shouted, "We beat 'em at their own game."

"It was somethin' for me to see," says Don Clemmons, today. "I had graduated by then but I useta go to all their games. When I was at Notre Dame Waldeyer would take me out if I got fancy. He never let my game open up. Then, I go to the games and see Frank going behind his back and Barry dribbling through his legs."

"Okay, let's make it stick," says Frank now. "John Waldeyer knows the game inside and out. But I have to question the way he deals with his players. He's cold. My grades were questionable in my senior year and his attitude seemed to be that once the season was over, that was it. I wasn't on top at the time, so I had to pull myself along. I can't point to any adult who helped me."

"Yeh," adds Barry McLeod, "Waldeyer knows as much as any coach I ever saw. He's a great mechanical coach. He helped us. But we helped him, too. We opened up his game. We helped him personality-wise, too. We were the first people like us—not your average Notre Dame students—he had to deal with. Near the end of the year he even asked us over to his house for sandwiches."

"I learned from Barry and Frank," says John Waldeyer. "I learned to coach less. When we got ahead by ten points, Barry would say, 'Whatcha say, Coach? Show time?' I'd let each of them do his own thing and they'd have fun. They even opened up more with me. One night they slept in my cellar with six of their black friends from the Terrace. Of course, they were hiding from the cops for some reason, but I don't know what. Barry opened up more to me than Frank. I remember when we lost the state semifinals to Harding, an all-black team composed of players mostly from Father Panik Village in the east end of Bridgeport, Barry actually cried on my shoulder. 'It ain't fair, Coach,' he kept crying. 'It ain't fair for us to lose to a bunch of junkies.'"

"Frank fouled out of that game," says Barry, "and I was in foul trouble the whole game. We both got around seventeen points I think. Frank and I felt so bad we walked home, about five miles. It was raining and snowing, but we didn't care. We just wanted to be by ourselves. We didn't go to school for two weeks. It's toughest when you lose a game against your own city guys. Those are the dudes who are important. You see them every day. If you lose you got to catch shit at the boys' club. If you lose to one of those upstate farmer teams, it don't matter. Who cares if some asshole from Simsbury throws in a two-hander at the buzzer to beat you? He don't even have a game, man. It don't mean nothing. They ain't guys you hang with."

After that loss in the state tournament their senior year, Frank and Barry waited for the college scholarship offers to come in. They knew they had been scouted that season, most heavily during the first Kolbe–Notre Dame game in which they had combined for forty-nine points and Walter Luckett had scored forty-eight, and now they wanted to see which scouts were interested in them. There was talk that Providence and Niagara wanted them, but still, a few weeks after the close of their season, they had heard nothing.

"Today, Barry and Frank are legends in Bridgeport," said Bruce Webster, "but at the time they were seniors in high school not everyone thought they were major college material. I knew they were, but I also knew there were problems. Especially with their grades." John Waldeyer says of his two stars, "Academically Barry was slower than Frank, but he got better grades. Frank was sharper, but he only did what he had to in order to play basketball."

"My grades were bad but Barry's were worse," disagrees Frank. "Bad to worse, I guess. I had to take the college boards twice because I didn't predict. The scouts would all tell me they'd love to have me but my grades were bad. They said if I was black it would be okay, because they could get me in. I thought that was a fucked-up situation, man."

John Waldeyer recalled an incident that he feels best exemplifies the frustration his two players felt. A week before the end of the season they had one of their better games and waited with great anticipation for the weekly scholastic basketball magazine devoted to a rundown of the top prospects in the country. Each week they devoured that magazine, waiting expectantly for their names. Each week they read of Walter Luckett's latest exploits. This particular week they were sure they would get some mention, until they examined the magazine before a game and found they were not even in it. Barry flung the magazine across the locker room and snapped, "Shit, no one wants us! We got no publicity! Look at Luckett!"

Both Frank and Barry felt that Walter Luckett's prolonged stardom over four years had robbed them of their rightful share of the limelight. So many scouts had been dazzled by Walter's brilliance for so long that they were blinded to the talents of a host of lesser stars like Frank and Barry. In any normal year, without a Walter Luckett, Frank and Barry would have been sought after by most college scouts. There was a ring of truth to their claim. At one point during the year Digger Phelps, the head basketball coach at Notre Dame University, had traveled to Bridgeport to see Walter Luckett play. He arrived too late to see Luckett, but was told that if he waited around for an hour or so he could see another, slightly less talented player: Frank Oleynick. Phelps said, "I'm not interested in any trash," and returned to South Bend, Indiana.

However, Frank and Barry had also benefited from Walter's publicity in a way most evident the night of the first Notre Dame–Kolbe game. Walter brought the scouts to see him, and inevitably that night they got to see Frank and Barry, two players they probably never would have seen without the Luckett drawing card. It seems that Frank and Barry were both cursed and blessed by Walter's brilliance, and in their senior year this began to obsess them. At one time Luckett had been their idol and they had emulated him. "They hate to admit it," says junior varsity coach Dave Bike, "but they both tried to shoot like Walter." Then he had become a goal, something to strive for as proof of their own emerging talent. And now, in their senior year, he was a curse. "Frank's overriding concern as a senior was to be better than Walter Luckett," says John Waldeyer. "He started calling him 'The Big Jig.'"

With their senior year about to come to a close, Frank and Barry still had no concrete scholarship offers, and they began to panic. For the first time in their lives, and possibly too late, they began to realize they had to get out of Bridgeport, away from both family and friends.

"A friend of mine had just died from an overdose," says Barry.

"We had to get out of the Port," adds Frank. "We had to escape our surroundings. Drugs. Trouble. Everything was stagnant. I saw players who were better than me and they were still there. Doing nothing. Why hadn't they escaped, I wondered? They were better than me. I kinda panicked. I thought those guys might be me. At the time I couldn'ta cared less about studies—basketball was my whole life—but I studied hard the second time I took the college boards."

Part of Frank and Barry's problem was that because of their background and black associations, many scouts were scared of them. Those scouts felt the two had been so closely tied to the black experience that they inevitably must have been tainted by it. How could they move in such a world without being infected by its drugs and despair? The fears were unfounded, however, since Frank and Barry both had the strength of character and the intelligence to take only what was best for them from the ghetto. They took out their basketball skills and some close friendships, and left to the ghetto its drugs and hopelessness. Today, looking back, Barry wonders out loud, "Were we carpetbaggers?"

In contrast to the accepted behavior for most young white athletes, the attitudes of Barry and Frank could be seen as forbidding. After all, it took the constant ministrations of a Notre Dame priest just to coax them through their four stormy years at the high school. "His name was Father Beaupre," says Barry. "He tried to understand us."

"He gave me money," says Frank. "He saw something in us. He carried me through school. I never ran into people like that before. He never asked for anything. I kept waiting. I questioned his angle." It was this basic cynicism of Frank's that may have scared off many of the college scouts who came to see him play. He was cynical beyond his years, but not beyond his experience. As Barry put it, "We've seen things in our school days that most people never see in 100 years."

This cynicism erupted in frequent fights with their peers, which often had more damaging results than mere bruises. One particular fight almost cost Barry and Frank a chance to go to college and conceivably could have cost them their lives. During the summer before their senior year, Frank and Barry played for the Beardsley Terrace team in the Summer Parks Recreational Basketball League. One of their fiercest rivals was the team from P. T. Barnum Apartments in the south end. P. T. had its own white star in a black field, Phil Nastu. He would go on to become a small-college All-American basketball player, and is presently a successful minor league baseball pitcher in the San Francisco Giant's organization. But then, in the summer of 1972, he was one of Frank and Barry's bitterest rivals. He, too, had a certain notoriety as a white youth playing a black game among blacks.

"Before our game," says Frank, "Nastu drives by the Terrace with some of his gang. He points a finger out the window and says he's gonna do this and this and this to us when we go over to P. T. for the game. We knew it wasn't gonna be a game, just a fight. We were the only whites on our team, and Nastu was the only white dude on his team. On the day of the game, on the very first play, I threw the ball in Nastu's face."

"Yeh," says Barry, "and on the next play my brother Ron goes up for a shot and Nastu fouls him. Ron turns around and slugs Nastu and knocks him down. Me and Frank come running, and we both jumped on Nastu and started punching him. We were in P. T., but his friends just watched. Our friends from the Terrace held them off with cans of Mace. Somehow Nastu's ankle got broken. We were lucky to get out of there with our lives."

"That fall, after we beat Kolbe in the first game before all those scouts," says Frank, "we were going to go over to the south end to play Nastu's high school team, Bassick. Before the game I got called into the principal's office at Notre Dame. They told me my mother had been getting threatening telephone calls all day: 'If your son goes to Bassick, you won't see him again.' Barry's mother got calls too. She was hysterical. Waldeyer had a meeting with the school principal, and they didn't want us to play the game. We told them we wanted to. Anyway, at the game my father had some friends of his who were cops. Barry and I had bodyguards. They followed us even to the bathroom. There were fifteen plainclothes cops at the game. The head cop says, 'Don't worry, we've got plenty of protection.' My father says, 'We don't want the guy *after* Frank gets shot!' We told them we were gonna play the game (we had our reps to protect) but there was no way we weren't gonna be scared."

"Well, we walked into the Bassick gym, and this is the God's honest truth, the fans had five tombstones with the names of our starting players on them. They had Barry's and my tombstones holding hands. Now, you got to remember this was the same week Luke Witte of Ohio State got stomped on by those Minnesota players. Before our game we were looking at pictures of that fight in *Sports Illustrated*. When we finally got on the court I played one of the worst games of my career. Barry wasn't much better. And that was the game *Cage World* magazine decided to scout us! Early on one of our players, Keith Lewis, slugs Nastu in the back. Me and Barry ran over to Keith and told him to cool it. 'Shit, we be the first ones to get it if there's any trouble,' we told him."

"The funny thing is," adds Barry, "now we're real good friends with Nastu. We even went to his wedding. Sometimes you regret things you do as kids."

"Well, that whole Nastu thing almost ruined it for both of us as far as college scholarships were concerned," says Frank. "One of the area coaches who was trying to help us out, Jack Kvancz, who played for Bob Cousy at Boston College, called us up real pissed off after that summer Nastu fight. He says, 'I got college scouts all over the country calling me about you, and what am I gonna tell them? I got two hoodlums?' "

Finally, during the summer after their graduation, Frank and Barry received their first firm scholarship offers. Frank's arrived first. It came from Seattle University, Elgin Baylor's alma mater. Dave Bike, who had just been named an assistant basketball coach at Seattle, had convinced the school's head coach, Bill O'Connor, to take a chance on Oleynick. Bike told O'Connor that he thought he could help handle Frank at that school, but even he doubted that he could handle both Frank and

Barry at the same time. In fact, most college coaches felt the same, that together Frank and Barry, no matter how talented they might be, would constitute a real headache for any team they might play on together. At the time he received that scholarship offer, Frank Oleynick was only sixteen years old.

Shortly after that, John Waldeyer told Barry that he had received word from Centenary College in Shreveport, Louisiana, that they were interested in him. Their assistant coach said he was traveling to Bridgeport to see Barry play in a summer outdoor Urban Coalition League game. The game was played at Nannygoat Park, a grassless oasis in the black, Spanish and Italian section of the city. Frank, Barry and Walter Luckett were all on the same team. Since Frank and Walter already had their college scholarships, they made a point of sacrificing themselves during the game for Barry. They passed up easy shots and fed the ball to him all game long, and Barry responded with a forty-point performance. A few days later he was on a plane to Shreveport to look over the school.

One of the first people he met at Centenary was a seven-foot black freshman named Robert Parish. "He was the biggest dude I'd ever seen," says Barry. Parish, who would become Barry's roommate and his closest friend except for Frank, was the reason Centenary coach Larry Little was interested in Barry. He told Barry that he needed a slick-passing guard to feed Parish the ball. He also told Barry it would require a drastic transition from being a shooting guard to a passing one. He wondered if Barry could submerge his ego enough to make that sacrifice for Parish and the team. Barry said he did not doubt that he could do it, especially if there was the possibility of a National Collegiate Championship at stake. "I'd always been on winning teams," says Barry. "That's all that matters to me. Frank and Walter were always out for the glory. I've always made my teams winners."

Barry did not think Frank could have made such a sacrifice. It was not in his nature, for one thing. For another, he had been deprived of personal glory for so long—longer than Walter or Barry—that now he was on its threshold he could not surrender its possibility. He had perfected his talent by a sheer act of will, and he was not about to submerge the result of all that hard work for anyone or anything. Quite to the contrary, Frank had begun to believe that he had far from perfected his talent, and that his tremendous willpower could carry him to greater personal achievements.

When Barry returned to Bridgeport, he and Frank prepared to leave the city and their families. It was something they looked forward to. Despite initial apprehension about leaving one another after all they had been through together, they looked forward to that as well. They had been too close too long, had become so identified one with the other in people's eyes that now they were eager to branch off on their own and satisfy the demands of their individual egos.

Barry's mother tried to allay his fears over leaving his cousin. "She told me not to worry about leaving Frank," says Barry. "She said he could take care of himself, that he was always only out for himself. Then she said, 'Frank will become a professional basketball player someday. You might become a professional too, but even if you don't, you'll make a great coach. Frank could never coach. He's too selfish.' I thought about what she said, but I wasn't sure she was right about Frank. Still, I knew Frank had done things to get where he was that I wouldn't have done. I also wondered about this quality I had that my mother saw."

five

Unlike Frank and Barry, Walter Luckett had no difficulty getting a college scholarship offer in his senior year of high school. His biggest problem was sifting through the over 200 offers he received to find the one he most wanted. The reasons for Walter's windfall were obvious. He was far more talented than either Frank Oleynick or Barry McLeod, and that talent had been sustained over a period of four years. Frank and Barry's talent had surfaced only in their senior year and so was still suspect as far as many of the college scouts were concerned. Walter's talent had also emerged sooner because he was a year older than Barry and two years older than Frank. He was taller too, and according to Frank and Barry he had had all the right breaks throughout his high school career.

When Walter first enrolled at Kolbe it was a small high school with no sports reputation. Its basketball schedule was dotted with the kind of small "farmer schools," as Barry put it, that could barely field a basketball team. So while Frank and Barry played freshman and junior varsity ball in their first two years at Notre Dame, which had one of the toughest basketball schedules in the state, Walter was averaging sixteen points a game for the Kolbe varsity his freshmen year playing against such teams as Ridgefield, Old Saybrook and Farmington. In his sophomore year Walter averaged around thirty points a game (he scored fifty-six against Abbot Tech) against the same caliber of competition. By the time Kolbe upgraded its schedule in his junior year to include all the tough city teams such as Notre Dame and Central, Walter had matured enough against the lesser teams to continue to star. Furthermore, in the space of one summer Walter had grown almost three inches, so the youth who had been only marginally taller than Frank and Barry (Walter was 6-1 to their 5-10) now seemed like a giant at 6-3. In his junior year Walter continued to score his thirty points a game, although not with the same regularity he had the previous year. (Against a tough Central team his junior year Walter was limited to only sixteen points.)

"Walter was lucky," says his best black friend, Warren Blunt. "He was older than everybody else and everything just seemed to fall in place for him. I was almost as good a basketball player as him in grammar school—I was even predicted as a high school All-American when I went to Central. But I hurt my shoulder, and then I didn't grow like Walter." Today Warren Blunt stands about 5-10 and weighs over 200 pounds.

Nor, like Frank and Barry, did Walter have trouble fitting into the social fabric at Kolbe. He was loved and respected by most of the school's white lay teachers and friars, who saw in his model deportment the kind of black youth they hoped to get a reputation for molding in the inner-city school. Walter was personally neat and was respectful to all the white adults at the school, which naturally drew them to him. They were also drawn because of the basketball talent he exhibited so early in his high school career. They latched on to Walter in the same way shrewd major league pitching coaches latch on to successful pitchers. Such coaches are always seen working with a player who is successful so that it appears to their front office that the pitcher's success stems from that coach's attention, and not the reverse.

Angelo Nocciolli, Walter's white godfather, says of the youthful Walter, "He was a hero to all the whites in the state. All the college scouts loved his attitude. They didn't like Frank's or Barry's, though. The scouts could relate to Walter in a way they couldn't relate to the cousins or to most black athletes." Ironically, Walter related more easily to whites, especially adults who had taken an interest in him, than to blacks. Frank's and Barry's lives were dominated by their black peers. In fact, whenever Frank, Barry and Walter got together to play basketball in the ghetto, invariably the blacks of the ghetto seemed to root more strongly for Frank and Barry than for Walter. A perfect example of this inverted allegiance to the two white youths, and Walter's confusion as to where his allegiance should lie, occurred in the summer of their respective senior years in high school. All three youths were to play in a Beardsley Terrace Urban Coalition League game against a touring black team headed by Marvin Barnes, then a star with Providence College. The game was played outdoor at night under lights before several thousand black residents from the Terrace, all of whom convened as if for a summer festival.

One wall of the outdoor court was solid concrete, painted black with a green and red outline map of Africa. Before the game began, each team lined up along the sidelines at respectful attention and faced that concrete wall in preparation for the playing of the national anthem. Mr. Nocciolli, who was there, describes the scene: "Me, my wife and my two kids were there along with Dr. Yanity and his wife and Mr. and Mrs. Luckett. We were the only whites among all those blacks. We were standing on the sidewalk alongside the court. There were bloodstains on the sidewalk where two girls had stabbed a guy the night before. We stood together, we didn't wander around. There were no incidents. At the time Marvin Barnes was into a black power thing and I could see he was wearing an earring. Before the national anthem was played, he went around to all the players on his team and made a point of raising their clenched fists in the air in a black power salute. Then he did the same with all the blacks on the Terrace team. He didn't bother with Frank or Barry, though. When he got to Walter, I could see Walter was hesitant to raise his hand. His hand was half up. He looked timid. He looked around at me, and then to Barnes."

Before the anthem was played, three small black boys walked to the center of the court carrying a folded flag, which, when rung up a flagpole, turned out to be emblazoned with the map of Africa. The anthem, played with almost all the players and the fans standing with their right fists clenched and raised in salute, was the song "In the Ghetto" by black singer Donnie Hathaway.

One reason Marvin Barnes did not raise Frank Oleynick and Barry McLeod's fists was because the two were white; the other reason was that both youths had raised their clenched fists voluntarily. They were the favorites of the 3500 fans and the game's announcer, whose name was Harrison Taylor.

"His nickname was the Fox," says Frank. "He had a lot of respect in the city. He was a fighter. He'd do a play-by-play thing during the game. He called Walter 'Doctor,' and he called me and Barry 'Butch Cassidy and The Sundance Kid.' He'd say to the fans, 'Now, they may look like they're white, brothers, but they ain't. You just watch them play. You've seen 'em go between their legs. You ever see a white boy go between his legs? I know 'em from way back. They're half black. They're my boys.' "

"His favorite line," says Barry, "was, 'I knew them when they was poor.' "

"That night we really turned 'em out," says Frank. "We beat the Barnes team by thirty points. He couldn't believe it. After the game they had a dance on the court with the music blaring so loud you could hear it all the way to Chamberlain Avenue."

"Man, we would get high off that music," adds Barry. "Sometimes at home I can still hear it."

Mr. Nocciolli remembers only that the Terrace won and that Walter took a lot of jump shots far from the basket. "He seemed afraid to go to the basket," he says. "Frank and Barry went to the basket often."

Walter admits that he was never the darling of the black community in Bridgeport. He says, "The blacks in Bridgeport looked on me as something different. The whites had a claim on me. It's funny, but whites never liked Frank. He did his thing alone. He was a cocky dude. He didn't give nobody no respect. I'll tell you one thing about Frank, he let's you know where he's coming from. He don't try to impress nobody. But he's a little nuts. At Notre Dame they called him 'nigger lover' and he tried to fight them all. He dated black girls, and the whites didn't like that. The blacks admired him for it. It's funny, you know, but Frank is a lot tied up with my career. The game I scored my thousandth point, Frank split my eye open on a rebound. I helped him a lot in high school. I got him to play with me, and I told him he should shoot more at Notre Dame. I'd cuss him out when he'd pass. He'd listen to me. He always told me I helped him a lot. At the first Kolbe–Notre Dame game, O'Connor, the Seattle U. coach, was there to recruit me, and when I told him I wasn't going to Seattle he picked up Frank. I was responsible for Frank's career. Barry's, too. We were the baddest. The three of us would go into a bar in Bridgeport and laugh and say, 'You got the three purest shooters in the nation here.' "

If Walter Luckett's first three years at Kolbe were without tension, his final year was not. A sustained assault was launched upon him by college coaches, friends, hangers-on and even members of his own family, all of whom were trying to influence his choice of college. (His father threw him out into the snow once in the middle of such an argument.) That tension had a decided effect on his playing: his scoring average dropped from over forty-five points per game at the beginning of the season to thirty-nine points per game at the close, and he lost the national high school scoring championship by a few percentage points to John Drew, presently a star with the Atlanta Hawks of the National Basketball Association. But the stress had an even more deleterious effect on his psyche, which would not be clearly evident until well into his college career.

From the beginning of his senior year, it was obvious Walter was one of the best players in the nation.

Hundreds of college coaches descended on him and his family. They followed him everywhere, with as many as forty attending each of his high school games. After those games the coaches wined and dined Walter and his family. "Sometimes Walter preferred to go off with his friends," says Angelo Nocciolli, his godfather, "so the coaches would take just me and Mr. and Mrs. Luckett out to dinner. Most of the time, though, they tried to isolate Mr. Luckett. They knew about his drinking. They'd tell me to leave and then they'd try to get him drunk. They'd say, 'Mr. Luckett's gonna stay here with us for a while,' and I'd say, 'That's all right with me, but I'll tell you one thing. Anything Mr. Luckett says about the kid don't mean nothing, 'cause the kid's gonna decide where he wants to go.' What they didn't know was that Mr. Luckett had asked me and George Fasolo to help him out with all this recruiting."

The scouts finally realized this when Fasolo was quoted in a local newspaper story as saying, "When the choice of school is made it will be one carefully picked to guard Walter against being hurt in any way, to assure that his course of study will not represent too tough a load, and to provide that he will play under a good coach."

"After awhile," continued Mr. Nocciolli, "when they got the picture, the scouts started working on me too. They used the religious thing with me. They knew I was religious. I'll tell you, they'd use anything to get the kid. They'd sell their souls. One night in Plainville, Connecticut—Walt's whole family was there—the coaches offered him anything he wanted. When they saw I had driven Mr. Luckett there, they went out to my car and put a case of booze in it for him. I could tell this kind of story a hundred times over. Mr. Luckett loved the recruiting, though. He was offered a new house, food, everything by the recruiters, but he turned it all down. I told him, 'Don't sell your son for money.' He said, 'Don't worry, I won't. These guys think they got me with a little booze, but I'll drink 'em all under the table.' And he did.

"But I'm afraid the one bad thing that came out of it all was Mr. Luckett's realization that he could use people. One time, when Walt was coming back from a recruiting trip, Mr. Luckett called me up and told me to pick up Walt at LaGuardia Airport. I told him he was crazy. This kinda thing rubbed off on Walt, too. He also began to use people. He'd get the assistant coach at Kolbe, Warren Canfield, to drive him all over town. He even asked my son, who was in his class, to help him with an upcoming math test one time. I told my kid it was all right. Then, whenever my kid tried to tell Walter something, Walt wouldn't listen. Finally I went into the room and told Walt to shut up. I told him my son couldn't carry his bags as an athlete, but that he didn't have my kid's brains either, so he'd just better listen to him. He did and he got an 87 on the test. But I can't be too hard on Walter. After all, he felt more pressure in one year than my kid ever would in his whole lifetime."

Once the high school season was concluded and Walter still had not chosen his college, the mounting pressure began to take its toll. At the time he had been picked to play in a number of post-season high school all-star games, all of which he easily should have starred in. But he did not. He prepared for one of those games, the Dapper Dan Classic in Pittsburgh, by playing one-against-one with his friend Frank Oleynick. Frank says of those practices, "There was still no real competition between me and Walt at that time. I was just trying to help him get into shape. We played hard, but there was no ego thing involved. He didn't fear me as a rival then, but he did have respect for my game."

That respect had grown when the two players, along with Barry McLeod, had gone together to Danbury, Connecticut, to compete in a post-season tournament. Frank and Barry scored almost as many points as Walter (in the twenties to his thirties), and the disparity between their respective talents seemed far less great than it had been during the high school season only a few weeks before. They got along well too, even in the face of adversity. After the game, it seems Walter's ramshackle car was stolen. Frank, Barry and Walter were left without a ride back to Bridgeport. The sponsor of their team, the owner of an Italian Importing Company, appeared in a long, dark Cadillac. He offered to drive the boys back to Bridgeport, but before he did he'd ask a few friends if they couldn't find Walter's car. Walter remembers sitting in the back of the Cadillac with Frank and Barry while the owner fumed. "He was cussing," says Walter. "He said, 'Some sumabitch taka de car, I killa sumabitch.' Me, Frank and Barry were scared to death. Frank said, 'Shit, we be with a buncha gangsters.' Well, he musta gave somebody the kiss of death because in twenty minutes we got my car back."

Walter Luckett, the second leading schoolboy scorer in the nation, scored only fourteen points at the Dapper Dan Classic, a disappointment to most of his Bridgeport fans who had made the trip to Pittsburgh. One of those fans, Mr. Nocciolli, says, "He coulda scored thirty points but he wouldn't shoot the ball. I couldn't understand it at first, and then the next game he went to at Howie Garfunkel's Five-Star Camp, he did the same thing. You woulda had a tough time picking Walter out at that game. He got only eleven points and he repeatedly passed the ball off to Phil Sellers, who would go on to become an All-American at Rutgers. Sellers got twenty points, and he was nowhere near the shooter Walter was. I think Walter gave up his shots because he was away from home with strangers for the first time, and more than anything he wanted to be liked by them and accepted. He'd always had this conflict between being a star and being liked, and when he had to choose one or the other, he always chose the latter." Mr. Nocciolli added that this conflict surfaced during these all-star games and would carry through for the rest of his life.

Walter Luckett's life, to that point, had been defined by others, particularly white adults. At first Mr. Fasolo, Mr. Nocciolli and Dr. Yanity had been the strongest influences, even more so than his own father. Then, with the arrival of the college recruiters, most of whom were also white, Walter again turned to white adults for approval. In fact, often during a high school game he would heed a college coach's request to exhibit a certain aspect of his talent, such as passing or dribbling, by emphasizing that aspect at the expense of his shooting. He began to play to the scouts' wishes. Because for so long he had been influenced by white adults, Walter was eager to listen to this new group who were taking control of his life. Once he moved away from Bridgeport and there was no one to advise him, as at these various all-star games, he found it hard to act. He looked for someone to tell him what to do, or how to play. And when there was no one, he became increasingly passive on the court.

Without people to reinforce his belief in himself and his talent, a belief that rested precariously on external approval, Walter had no belief in himself. Since he was the creation of others and not his own (in contrast to Frank Oleynick and Barry McLeod), once he was away from the major influences on his life he found it increasingly difficult to function.

Kenny Sumpter, another of Frank, Barry and Walter's black friends, is the youth who predicted that Walter would have to outscore both Frank and Barry combined for Kolbe to beat Notre Dame in their senior year. He says this of the Walter Luckett he saw late that year: "Walter started changing his course in his senior year of high school. I remember one game, the New York–Connecticut All-Star game in Bridgeport, when it was most obvious to me. Walter was more conscious of passing the ball than shooting it. I don't know who talked him into that, maybe the college recruiters. But anyway, here he is, first-team All-American in his own home town, and he don't even take the MVP award. That was the worst sign. I said to him after the game, 'Man, you only got twelve points! Where'd you get this idea you got to pass the ball?' He wouldn't say nuthin' to me. From then on he was more conscious of what people thought of him rather than what he was doing himself. But when *I'd* tell him what he should be doing, he don't want to hear it. Only from certain people. He wants his friends, like me and Clem, to tell him how good he looked. I tried to let him realize I was always pulling for him, but whenever I criticized his game, he wouldn't understand.

"Walter began to lose his confidence somewhere. Before, he couldn't wait to shoot. Now there was hesitation. You had to force him to shoot. Maybe it was all this pressure on him. It never affected him until his senior year. Maybe he was so much in the limelight it blew his mind. I'd always thought he had this built-in confidence, like when we'd go to a party all he'd talk about was what he's gonna do next game. Now he be talking about how lousy somebody else is. It seems he didn't want to do nuthin' on the court anymore.... You know how a little boy is? He can be so innocent. He'll do anything. He's not aware of how people look at him. He's not self-conscious. Well, Walter suddenly got aware people were looking at him and he lost that innocence."

A number of factors affected Walter's final choice of college, but the primary one was his suddenly emerging insecurity. He began to question his talent only when it dawned on him that he would have to leave all those people who had spent their lives reinforcing his belief in that talent. Without them, Walter would be lost. No matter how many points he scored, no matter how many accolades he received, no matter that his high school uniform was retired in the Springfield, Massachusetts, Basketball Hall of Fame, Walter still only believed of himself whatever the last person told him. Once away from those friendly boosters such as Nocciolli, Fasolo and Yanity, he would be thrown back on himself. He either had to choose new confidants or stand alone. This would greatly determine his college selection.

Walter immediately eliminated all southern colleges from his list of potential schools. He did not want to undergo the pressures that would be thrust on him as a prominent black in a white-dominated racist environment. He also eliminated all black-dominated schools, such as Grambling College in Grambling, Louisiana, and those other integrated schools known for the excessive racial pride of their black students.

"Walter was always turned off by schools he visited that had special black orientation days just for him," says Mr. Nocciolli. "One school marched some blacks around the cafeteria to impress him with their black consciousness. Another school had him talk with their most prominent black militant. This guy ripped his school and told Walter that all the blacks there wouldn't have anything to do with the school's social life, but preferred to go across the tracks to the ghetto instead. Walter didn't like that idea one bit."

Walter Luckett's idea was to escape the ghetto and Bridgeport, not simply to find a distant substitute for them. He said, "I wanted to get away from the ghetto environment. Maybe go to the country. Hell, there was fighting every day where I lived. My brothers carried knives just to protect themselves. I got beat up more than my share. Maybe it was healthy for me at the time. But still I had to get away. There was no privacy. People were always on my bandwagon."

Walter chose not to go to a college too far distant from Bridgeport, such as Seattle University, where he would not be within at least a day's drive from home. He eliminated those schools whose style of play was not conducive to his own. Since he played a cautious, almost suburban game, this eliminated such run-and-gun schools as Oral Roberts and the University of Nevada at Las Vegas. And finally, and most importantly, Walter would not go to a college where he could not star immediately. This eliminated such powerhouses as Maryland, UCLA and Providence, all of which were eager to recruit him.

"Walter was always askin' me what school he should go to," says Don Clemmons. "I'd say, 'Providence.' They got a history of guards going to the NBA. It was in the East. It was close to home and still far enough away for him to be on his own. But he'd say, 'If I go to Providence next year, they still got DeGregorio. And Barnes is a junior. And Stacom is transferring from Holy Cross.' I say, 'But you better than Stacom right now. You just gotta show 'em. Even if you don't start your first year, you won't be no worse than sixth man.' But he wanted to be a star right away. He say, 'Yeh, yeh, but they still got DeGregorio.' I say, 'So what, you'll all get it together and work out a good team.' He say, 'Yeh, yeh,' but still he didn't want to have nothin' to do with Providence. And look what happens. Providence goes to the NCAA semis that year and Luck would have been a freshman getting all that exposure."

Walter's selection was finally narrowed down to a major East Coast school in a pastoral setting with a predominantly white student enrollment where he would be an immediate star on its basketball team. Preferably it would be one whose reputation in basketball had always been modest, so that Walter Luckett could single-handedly transform their program into one of national prominence. He also preferred a school that had some ties with one of the men who had had some influence over his career and his life.

Such a school was Ohio University in Athens, Ohio, near the West Virginia border. It was Dr. Peter Yanity's alma mater, and a school that had been recruiting Walter (through Dr. Yanity) ever since he was in the eighth grade. He would be comfortable there. Safe. With Yanity's influence, he would feel he had an edge there—as if a player of his caliber needed such an edge. In Walter's mind Ohio U. was the perfect school for him. It was in the weak Mid-American Conference, never noted for its basketball strength, a conference in which Walter could immediately dominate. The school had not had a twenty-point-a-game scorer in its entire history. As Walter would tell a *Sports Illustrated* writer just before his picture appeared on that magazine's cover, "I'll get fifteen points just hanging around. . . ." Their coach, Jim Snyder, was a kindly, cautious man whose teams played a conservative, set up, work-for-the-good-shot type of offense, which Walter believed would be conducive for his long-range shooting style. Furthermore, he felt that Snyder was the kind of coach with whom he could have his own way.

"Ohio U. had 20,000 whites and 4000 blacks," says Walter. "It was the best thing that ever happened to me. It had a beautiful campus. It was a college town. No prejudices. No old people. It was open. Everything was green. Perfect, ya know? I was away from Bridgeport. I had my own apartment. The alumni treated me great. After every game I found $20 in my sneakers. I say to myself, 'Where am I, heaven?' In Athens, first of all, you don't have to worry about people breathing down your back, breaking into your home. I could look out my window and see cows grazing. I went horseback riding. It was heavy. I went to the lakes. Wild! It was country livin'. I dug it. It was never real cold. It was sweet. The people were so nice. People actually said hello to me on the streets. They had a smile on their face even if they didn't know I was a basketball player. In Bridgeport, in the ghetto, you walk down the street, you got to project an image. Super cool. Bad dude. You got to be in your ride half leaning out the window. You got to have a bitch with you. You got to act *bad*! But in Athens you don't have to go through that. I walked more than anything in Athens. I enjoyed walking! You don't walk in Bridgeport—you get busted in the side of the head if you look the wrong way. You got to be a tough black dude. That ain't my style. That's Frankie's style. My style is to be open. I like people."

But not everyone who liked Walter Luckett in his senior year of high school thought his choice of Ohio U. was the best for him and his career. One of those doubters was Don Clemmons. He claims that it was Walter's attempt to stack the deck in his favor that made him choose Ohio U. "His main reason for going there was to be in the limelight right away," says Clemmons. "There were no stars there. But that wasn't good for him. He was so worried about having to share the limelight that he didn't want me to go with him to Ohio, either. At the time I was averaging twenty-five points a game for a junior college. Dr. Yanity said he liked my game. He said he thought he could get me and Walt a package deal at Ohio U. For months Walt kept saying, 'If I go, you gonna go, too.' He say it so much, he act like he be serious. Then when it got out around Bridgeport that I might be going too, people began saying to me, 'If you go out there, maybe you be the man instead of Luckett.' Walt didn't like that. He began to see me as a threat. He didn't want to share his glory. But I would have accentuated his game. I'd be a set-up guard for him. Walt say, 'Yeh, yeh, you be my set-up.'

But then he stopped talking about me going with him. Things kinda died down, and then he didn't even tell me when he announced to the papers he was going to Ohio U."

Shortly after Walter Luckett told the world that he would attend Ohio University on an athletic scholarship, *Sports Illustrated* sent a reporter and a photographer to the Athens, Ohio, campus to record his arrival. The magazine's November 27, 1972, issue featured a photograph of Walter Luckett on its cover and a long rambling story inside, the gist of which was that Walter Luckett was probably the best freshman basketball player in the country at the time. Walter himself seemed to agree with that estimate of his prowess. He was quoted as saying, among other things, that last season's Ohio U. team "stunk on ice" and, with his arrival in Athens, that state of affairs would soon be remedied. "They get the ball to me in our two-guard front," he was quoted as saying, "and I will positively freak. I mean, I will drive those rascals wild." He did conceded, however, that scoring forty points a game, as he had done so effortlessly in high school, was a rather unrealistic goal for him to aim at. But, he added, "I'll tell you this. I'm shooting it. I'll get fifteen just hanging around. . . ." To anyone who had seen Walter play in high school, this was not an idle boast. Even his former rival from Notre Dame, Barry McLeod, did not doubt that Walter would easily score over fifteen points a game. "Why not?" said Barry. "He's Walter Luckett. His picture was on the cover of *Sports Illustrated*. I mean, one week Walter Luckett, the next Muhammad Ali. I was in the Centenary library when I saw his picture on the magazine rack. I went wild. I stole the magazine and ran to show it to my teammates. 'That's my man!' I said. 'The man I been telling you about!' "

In his freshman year at Ohio U., Walter Luckett averaged thirteen points a game. Opposing fans booed him and threw pennies at him on the court. His own fans booed him. His teammates disliked him and disparaged his talent. Walter cried often that year and longed to return to Bridgeport. Over the next two years his play improved considerably. He averaged almost twenty-five points a game, was named to a number of All-American teams as an honorable mention and was even named Most Valuable Player in the Mid-American Conference in his sophomore year, when his team won the league title.

Yet Walter Luckett would never fulfill the potential his talent once hinted at when he was in high school. In fact, many of the people who had seen him play during his earlier years claimed that far from improving, or even merely stagnating, Walter Luckett actually deteriorated as a player during his college career. "Walter was never again as good as he was in high school," said Kenny Sumpter, echoing the sentiments of Don Clemmons and a host of Walter's old friends who were so sorely disappointed in Walter's choice of colleges and the effect it would have on his career. The reasons for that effect are many.

Before Walter enrolled at Ohio U. he injured his left knee during practice prior to one of his last high school games. Over the summer it was operated on. The knee healed slowly, and by the time basketball practice began at Ohio U., it still caused Walter considerable pain and greatly impaired his mobility. But since Ohio U. had invested so much in him and was so hungry for the success the school was sure he would bring, he was rushed into action. Walter, ever anxious to please, allowed himself to be so abused despite the excruciating pain.

"Walter called me from Ohio after he had the knee operation," says Barry McLeod. "I felt sorry for him. He'd say, 'Barry, they're draining it every day. They're sticking needles in it. They're trying to get me ready too fast. It swells up after a game and they got to drain it. It hurts all the time.' He started crying. 'It's not like they told me, Barry,' he says. 'They're shooting me up with cortisone. I gotta get outta here!' I mean, he was getting two points a game. He's Walter Luckett! He's supposed to get fifteen points just walking out on the court. I remember watching him on TV with my teammates one afternoon. He looked bad. One guy says, 'He ain't nuthin.' I say, 'He's playing on only one leg, man. He's my man. He can play.' But they just kept cuttin' him up."

Despite the pain in his knee Walter played each game, and because he did the Ohio U. fans and players felt they had a right to expect him to produce as much as he had promised them. Since he was not living up to his braggadocio, they felt free to boo him unmercifully. His own teammates were particularly hard on him, as well they should have been after he was quoted as saying they "stunk on ice" without him.

"It's funny," says Dr. Yanity, "but Walter got along better with the whites than the blacks on the team. The blacks didn't like him. He was moody. One time he missed the team bus and they had to wait for him. He was always acting pouty, like a big-city dude. The problem was that the people who'd always kept Walter's ego under control were no longer there."

Though, if Walter no longer played like a star on the court, he continued to act like one off it. He was particularly hard on his mild-mannered coach, Jim Snyder.

"I cracked on the coach a coupla times," says Walter. "He didn't like it much but he had to come through. Once my car broke down, a raggedy old Pontiac. He gave me an even raggedier old Corvair that didn't have no brakes. I was driving home one day and the brakes went and I drove it right into a savings bank. I mean, right through the window. It was some small town with about 101 people and only two of them were black. I called up the coach and called him an s.o.b. I told him I wanted another motherfuckin' car right that minute. Oh, I cussed his ass out. He sent me a Vega."

If Walter was able to manipulate Snyder off the court, he did not have such luck on the court. Snyder had a conservative philosophy about the game. His team moved the ball deliberately, opting generally to work the ball underneath to one of the team's big men, none of whom could shoot as well ten feet away from the basket as Walter could from thirty. Most of the opposition—teams such as Toledo, Miami of Ohio and Bowling Green—were at best mediocre major college teams that played the same kind of controlled offense. During Walter's three seasons at Ohio U. his school posted consecutive records of 11–16, 18–9, 12–14. Often those teams scored less than sixty points a game. They played ponderous, plodding matches, more suited to a football field (for which most MAC schools are noted) than a basketball court. These games were difficult for Walter to adjust to, having come from the East where even high school teams played a slick, fast-paced game that resulted in over eighty points per side. No matter how deliberate

Walter's game might have seemed in the East, when compared to the slicker tactics of, say, Frank Oleynick and Barry McLeod, in the Midwest he seemed positively flashy in contrast to the Ohio U. style. Often Walter managed to get off less than fifteen shots a game (he hit over 60 percent of those shots), a far cry from the twenty-five or so shots he often managed in high school. Walter bristled at this kind of controlled action.

In his freshman year, playing with a bad knee, he was a point guard and was allowed to control the action somewhat. But since his mobility was impaired, he was often too closely guarded to free himself for a shot, and so had to pass off to a teammate. In his sophomore and junior years under Snyder and later his replacement, Dale Bandy, Walter was made a forward and no longer handled the ball as much. He stood around in the corner, clapped his hands and waited for a pass. Often his teammates ignored him. When he finally did get the ball he was frequently double-teamed, and because he was buried in the extreme corners of the court, he was unable to break free and make his own shot. To this day, he claims that if he had been a point guard in his junior and senior years, after his knee had completely healed, he would have been able to read the opposing team's defenses spread out before him and would have had the room, the entire half-court almost, in which to maneuver.

"I told the coach to let me handle the rock," Luckett says. "I told him I should be droppin' forty a game. He say I'm a head problem. He just didn't understand. Snyder wasn't really a bad guy, it was just he never even had a player who averaged twenty points a game, and here I am talkin' forty. All he ever say is, 'Work the power play to the big men. Work the power play.' I said to myself, I got to break this shit quick. But I couldn't. Snyder was a religious freak too. He was always prayin' before a game. 'The only way we win is with God,' he say. The guy who eventually replaced Snyder, Bandy, he promised me the world. He promised I'd handle the rock in my junior year, but I never saw it. I was stuck in the corner waitin' for the ball. I couldn't make things happen."

As a forward who did not handle the ball, Walter had to wait to receive it. Once he did, he had no operating room and he also had to contend with the opposing team's tallest men. Instead of trying to work his way through the opposition's defense (never his strong suit) for a lay-up, he began to take the easy way out. He either took long fadeaway jump shots or simply returned the ball to the team's point guard. His game became stagnant. His skills—ball handling, passing and graceful movement—began to deteriorate. Even his shooting fell off. He still managed to score twenty-five or so points a game and still managed excellent shooting percentages, but he was no longer the phenomenal-shooting, multifaceted talent he once had been.

As his skills deteriorated, so did his confidence. Although he claimed he could do things his coach would not let him do, he began to doubt, privately, that this was the truth. On those rare occasions when he did get breathing room and a chance to maneuver, he still opted for an easy long jump shot rather than trying to penetrate to the hoop. What he said he could do and what he actually did when he had the opportunity no longer bore any relation to one another. In fact, after Walter's knee healed he seemed disinclined to function as he once had. He seemed to have lost confidence after his disastrous freshman year in which he was booed. No matter how brazenly he talked, in reality it seemed that Walter really preferred to remain in the background, standing around, clapping his hands for the ball he never got. He seemed to take comfort in not getting the ball, in not having to prove himself again, as he had all his life, and in still being able to put the blame for his less than inspired play on his teammates and coaches. On the court he was almost timid. He admitted, "I lost my confidence."

Even before he went to Ohio, his friend Kenny Sumpter said, "Walt never knew how good he was. He only knew what other people told him." For example, when Walter was asked why he chose a nondescript school like Ohio U. instead of a more prestigious basketball school like UCLA, he said he would rather be a big fish in a small pond. He added that because of his knee injury he would be behind his teammates at Ohio in conditioning, but that they would wait for him to catch up because the team needed him.

"You think the big names [schools] would have done that?" he said. "Man, UCLA and Maryland have so many stars they'd forget me or send me home." This is a curious statement coming from the nation's second leading schoolboy scorer, whose picture was on the cover of *Sports Illustrated* and who, it was claimed, was one of the best freshman college players in the country.

At Ohio during his first year, people told him he was a disappointment, that he was nowhere near as good as he had been touted to be. This had an effect on Walter. He began to doubt his talent. He disappeared on the court. He hid himself at times, and in the process his talent atrophied. He seemed, like the greenest rookie, to be more worried about doing something wrong that would come to the fans' attention than about affirmative action. He hid this insecurity with braggadocio off the court and complaints that his talent was being strangled by his coaches and teammates. But the truth of the matter was that Walter Luckett was tired of being Walter Luckett; he was tired of having to prove himself over and over again. He had been great for so long, greater than most could envision being, and now that greatness had become a burden he wanted to shuck. He was the fast gun in town grown tired of proving himself, trying to sustain his image by bluster instead of performance. But this was a difficult task, made harder by the fact that even in Walter's own home town, Bridgeport, his talent had become suspect. His friends began to question his ability too. Maybe he was not as good as they had thought. Maybe he was not the best player ever to come out of the city. And they pointed to the emerging talent of Frank Oleynick at Seattle University as proof that maybe Walter had been overrated all along and perhaps Frank, who had developed more slowly, was the real gem.

six

Frank Oleynick's early experiences at the University of Seattle were not much more pleasant than those of Walter Luckett at Ohio University. His attic apartment in a dilapidated old house in the black section of the city was described by Dave Bike, his former coach at Notre Dame High and now an assistant coach at Seattle, as depressing. But it was not so "depressing" to Frank Oleynick, who had seen a lot worse back in the ghettos of Bridgeport. As a matter of fact, Frank's early impressions of Seattle, an almost frustratingly spotless large city, were that even its slums were vastly preferable to those of Bridgeport. Frank's only friend, and his roommate, during his first few months in Seattle was Jess McGaffre, a tough black from Oakland, who once in the heat of a game kicked a referee in the rear end.

"Frank was awful lonely and miserable during those first few months," says Mark Kaufman, the radio broadcaster of all Seattle games, who eventually befriended Oleynick. "He lived on pancakes and Wonder bread as a freshman. There was never anything in his refrigerator but pancake batter. But he wouldn't ever ask for anything. If I, or one of the coaches, invited him to our house for dinner, he'd say, 'Maybe I'll stop by if I'm not busy.'

He was constantly sick too. Maybe it was partly the rainy weather all the time. He always had colds. His blood sugar was down. But still, he'd get up every morning at six o'clock and run six miles. Then he'd work out in the afternoon, and if there was no game, he'd go practice alone at night. His problem, at first, was he had no personality. And it didn't help that he was always with blacks."

John Birnley, one of Seattle's assistant coaches and a black, says of that early Frank Oleynick, "Nobody understood him, not the whites or the blacks. The whites didn't understand why he hung around with blacks, or at least tried to, and even the blacks were suspicious of him. They'd never met a white dude like him before. And as far as his playing went, he was too hard-nosed for all of them. Too competitive. He'd drop his head when they missed lay-ups. He once told a teammate that his problem, and the problem of all the Seattle players, was that when they watched the opposing team warm up or play, they were watching as spectators. 'I watch to learn something,' he said."

When Seattle's head coach, Bill O'Connor, a former All-American from Canisius College in upper New York State, approached him about his difficulty in getting along with his teammates, Frank said, "Who am I supposed to hang with? It's natural for me to gravitate to the blacks, but they don't take to me right now. And as far as the whites go, who am I supposed to hang with there? Rod Derline? He's from Lacey, Washington, and he ain't said a word in three years. Or Dick Gross? Why should I? He's starting ahead of me and I know I'm better than him."

Frank's comment about Gross, a not unusual complaint from a young athlete, hit on the crux of most of his early difficulties at Seattle. He was not playing, in fact he hardly played at all in his team's first ten games. "He was so frustrated," says Bike, "that he was gonna quit and go back to Bridgeport. Then he got into a game against New Mexico in front of 15,000 people, and the first thing he does when he gets the ball at half-court is travel. Then the next time he touches the ball he throws it out of bounds. O'Connor yanked him and sent him right back to the junior varsity. It was a bad J. V. program and Frank didn't belong there. In his first game he scored about forty points in a half, and the next day he's back with the varsity. Finally he got in a game against the University of Nevada at Las Vegas. He scored about fifteen points in less than a half."

The next game Seattle played, Frank Oleynick started and scored twenty-one points. He was a starter from then on at Seattle for the rest of his career. (He averaged 14.5 points per game as a sophomore.) With the beginnings of his success on the court came a lessening of his tensions and problems off the court.

He found that he had a lot in common with Coach O'Connor, now that he was starting. "Frank was in the right place at the right time with O'Connor," says Mark Kaufman. "The team wasn't going that well and O'Connor could afford to use Frank a lot. Eventually the exposure Frank got for himself would reflect on the team, giving it a kind of recognition it would never have received without him. Besides, Frank and O'Connor were perfectly suited to one another as far as their basketball philosophies went. O'Connor did not believe in a lot of weight programs and conditioning programs, which suited Frank just fine, since he took care of that stuff on his own. Nor did O'Connor believe in a lot of plays or drills during practice. He just gave the team the ball and let them play. And playing was what Frank loved most. O'Connor just turned him loose.

"They had other things in common too," continued Kaufman. "Neither of them had much interest in studies. O'Connor once said that if he had a top student in biology who had an interest in music, a girl friend and a desire to play basketball, he couldn't use him. He'd have too many interests, O'Connor said. O'Connor only had one: basketball was his life, and it was Frank's. O'Connor never put any pressure on Frank to do well in his studies. The tragedy is that in Frank's first semester as a freshman he was turned on by school. It was a challenge for him to prove he could do it. He got a 2.3 average, which was about a C, and I remember once he came to me with an English essay he'd written and asked me to discuss it with him. That was the last such discussion we would ever have. Once he proved his point, that he could cut it in school, and once he learned that O'Connor didn't care one way or another, Frank couldn't care less about studies. It was all very frustrating to Dave Bike, though, because he was the team's academic adviser. He was always on Frank's ass to do well."

"He could have done it academically," says Bike, "but then he became a star and quit trying. I was always disappointed that Frank never fulfilled his potential, either academically or as a person. For a kid who acted so cocky, he was terribly insecure. He didn't like it when you got close to the bone. He would act real hard-nosed until you fought him head-on, then he'd go into a shell. He'd get to a point in a debate and then just walk away. He was very selfish too. He'd come over to my house a lot and get down on the floor and play with my kids whenever he was looking for something. Maybe some kind of family relationship, I don't know. Then, if we had a disagreement, he'd become the hard athlete all of a sudden and we wouldn't see him for weeks at a time. I guess it was difficult for someone who had never lived with love to be able to form deep relationships with anyone.

"When he wanted to he could turn on the charm, though. I remember the way he used to charm the wife of Eddie O'Brien, our athletic director. She'd say to him, 'Frankie, are you hitting the books?' And he'd smile, tap a book lightly with his fingertips and say, 'Just tappin' them a bit, Mrs. O'Brien, just tappin' them.' But above all else, Frank had this tremendous willpower. He felt he could do anything he put his mind to, and I guess he could point as proof to his own career. Rob Silver, a teammate who sort of idolized Frankie and followed him around, once said he never saw a guy who said he was gonna do something and then did it the way Frankie did. I told Rob it would catch up with him, the first time he ran up against something he couldn't master. If he lost his talent, for instance, I was afraid he'd lose that confidence and then his limitations would be shown for what they were and it would all collapse."

John Birnley remembers going to grammar school with Muhammad Ali, then Cassius Clay, when they were both thirteen-year-olds. "One day the teacher asked us what we all wanted to be in life," says Birnley. "Cassius raised his hand and said, very serious, that he was gonna be the greatest heavyweight boxing champion in the world. The rest of the class laughed at him. But he was *serious*. Frank is a lot like Ali. He's a great admirer of him too. He's got pictures of him all over his room. Both men have this unbelievable confidence. They think they can will themselves into being whatever they want. And they're both great trainers of themselves. Frank is one of the few young players I ever met who knew how to practice alone. I used to open up the gym for Frank late at night and he'd spend hours going through solitary dribbling and passing drills. He'd throw the ball off the wall or set up game situations and play against an invisible opponent. He'd work on his game movements so that when he got into a game he'd just flow right with it. Sometimes we'd go one-on-one against each other. I'd try to make him play sound defense. Sometimes I'd ask him about his studies, too. He'd always smile at me and say, 'John, I came here for the season, not the reason.'"

Frank Oleynick's intense willpower, his perseverance, his good fortune at being in the right place at the right time and, above all, the benefit of all those years of practicing alone going back to his boyhood days on Pitt Street, had finally paid off for him. He averaged almost fifteen points a game as a freshman, and during his sophomore year (1974) upped that scoring average to twenty-five points a game, good enough to place him tenth in the nation. By the end of his sophomore year he was a virtual legend in Seattle, known throughout the city as "Magic" by the fans who had come to adore him.

"Frank saved basketball in Seattle," says Mark Kaufman. "The Sonics were going nowhere and Frank had turned on the city to the point where more people would go to watch him play than would go see the Sonics. He got the name 'Magic' partly because of the way he played. The fans on the West Coast never saw anyone dribble behind their back and through their legs like

Frankie did, and certainly they never saw a white guy play like him. But mainly he got his nickname because he won three games for Seattle with last-second shots at the buzzer. When he started this 'magic' streak the team was 2–7 and then they won thirteen of seventeen to finish 15–11, second in the West Coast Athletic Conference behind San Francisco. Seattle U. used to be called 'O'Brien Tech' because of the O'Brien brothers, and then it became 'Baylor Tech' because of Elgin Baylor. By the end of Frankie's sophomore year it was called 'Oleynick Tech.' "

"The people in Seattle who didn't know him loved him," says Dave Bike. "He had a baby face. He was smart enough to have short hair when everyone else was wearing it long. The press took a liking to him too, and he was a good interview. He always went to clinics and represented the school well. At the time, his hanging around with blacks didn't hurt him yet."

Frank Oleynick says of his early days in Seattle and his eventual canonization by the city's fans, "When I first got to the West Coast I was still into that East Coast con game. You know, you always gotta have an angle. Be cool, like in the Terrace. Man, there was this one record shop that was so trusting when I came in that before long I had stole over 200 records. But then it wasn't fun no more. It was no contest. After awhile I began to put my shields down. The people were so friendly. Casual. Eventually Seattle broadened me. It was the first time I had seen things could be better than the Terrace. Suddenly the Terrace didn't seem so cool anymore. Still, it was obvious from the way I dressed and talked that I was not from Seattle. When I started playing well the fans picked up on this. My background from Bridgeport began to get a lot of publicity in Seattle. I was just what the doctor ordered. The fans loved me. They were not used to a flamboyant, East Coast type of game, especially from a white dude—a lot of blacks go behind their backs. I stood out, and then too, I was lucky that my coach gave me a chance to do my thing. The attention I started to get in Seattle more than made up for the lack of attention I had received from whites in Bridgeport. But only from whites. My friends in the Terrace never questioned my ability. They knew what I could do.

"I even started getting into a little social life at Seattle. For the first time I started going out with a lot of white chicks. Back in Bridgeport, when I went out with white girls they were basically no different from the black chicks I went with. But in Seattle they were different. More friendly. Aggressive, really. You didn't need to give them no spiel to get them into bed. You know, it was no struggle to get their clothes off. Sex was the best ever in Seattle. My teammates used to see me arrive for practice and immediately go take a shower, and they couldn't understand why.

"I even got a girl friend there. She was white. At first, you know, I didn't treat her too good. I just used her. I wasn't used to somebody always giving like that. I thought she was a fool for being like that. Then I realized she was just a good person. But it's always been harder for me to make it with someone I care about. If I don't care for them, it's no problem. Her parents were millionaires. Her father was a stockbroker, and he really dug me. They lived in an English Tudor type of mansion out on Mercer Island. It was . . . oh . . . about as big as Building 16 in the Terrace. Of course, 400 families live in Building 16. They had a solarium, and there were more plants in it than there was grass in the Terrace. In the solarium they had some doves too. I'm not kidding. They had real live doves in the house. All night long you could hear them doves cooing to each other. Shit, if they was cooing in the Terrace they'd be on a spit in no time. . . . Yep, Seattle was the joint, man. You know, the jointsky. But it was no place like home."

Word of Frank Oleynick's Seattle success spread quickly throughout his native city. Each week the Bridgeport *Post-Telegram* carried a column devoted to the nation's leading collegiate basketball scorers. Frank's name, at one point, topped that list in his sophomore year, then settled comfortably in either the sixth or seventh spot for the entire year, while Walter Luckett's name could not be found until the twenty-second spot. Friends of both players wondered what had happened in the short space of two years to enable the Frank Oleynick they knew, a solid but unspectacular high school player, to surpass the exploits of Walter Luckett, once the most phenomenal schoolboy player in the country.

Walter Luckett began to wonder too. Now when he came home, his name was no longer the only one on Bridgeport fans' lips. For the first time in his life he had to share the limelight at home, and this had an adverse effect on Walter's career and his psyche. Frank had staked out a claim on what Walter had thought would always be his own private preserve. For the first time in their long friendship, an adult tension existed between the two. A rivalry developed that would be to Frank's advantage and Walter's disadvantage. For Frank Oleynick, it would become his goal to surpass Walter Luckett. While to Walter Luckett, Frank Oleynick would become an obsession that would haunt him and ultimately help destroy his career.

"When Frank realized that he was in the limelight too," says Don Clemmons, "it was a pivotal point in his career. His confidence grew against Luck. He had no animosity toward him, it was just that now he felt he could challenge Walter in the city."

"When we'd get back to Bridgeport," says Frank, "Walter and I would play against each other a lot. I'd try to kill him. I did sometimes. After our freshmen year we couldn't guard each other without a mental conflict coming out. Walter made me aware of this conflict first. I'd become a rival to him, someone in his class. I made the top freshman in my conference and averaged fifteen points a game. Walter averaged fifteen points a game too, but he was supposed to be the top freshman in the country. After our sophomore year, when it was evident the margin between us had closed, this ego thing got to the point where he'd never bring up anything positive about me. I felt hurt at first. Then I was embarrassed for him, like it was someone in my family hurting me. I don't even like to be talking about him like this, rivalry stuff. I don't want to do anything to hurt Walter. In a very serious way I began to feel sorry for him, that he had this attitude toward me.

"One day we were both supposed to play in a Rucker League game in New York. A lot of pros, like Tiny Archibald, were gonna be playing. I went riding all over Bridgeport looking for Walter but couldn't find him, so I went to New York without him. I had a nice game that day. I scored twenty or so points against Archibald. When word got around back in Bridgeport what I did, Walter started saying I didn't wait for him on purpose. He claimed I left him so I could be the whole show."

In another Rucker game that Walter went to on his own, Ken Sumpter says, "Luck made believe he wasn't taking it serious. Before the game he played to the crowd instead of warming up. He was just doing style for the fans instead of warming up serious. Frankie never noticed the fans when he warmed up. By then Walter was very conscious of people watching him. He seemed more conscious of people watching him than of playing the game. He had developed this little sideways look of his whenever he did something. He'd take a shot, then quick glance over his shoulder to see how people reacted to it. Frankie just put his head down and played."

If Frank Oleynick was beginning to assert himself against Walter Luckett, Walter did not let Frankie surpass him without firing off one last salvo in a game played during the summer before their junior year. Walter pulled himself together and played the kind of brilliant game he had regularly produced in high school but had failed to produce since. The game was staged in New Haven, at the city's new coliseum. It was billed as "John Williamson Day" in honor of the New Haven guard who had gone on to stardom with the New York Nets of the ABA. In addition to Williamson there was a host of NBA and ABA stars, among them Earl Monroe, Calvin Murphy and the incomparable Julius Erving. Every one of Oleynick and Luckett's friends who attended that game admit the same thing: Julius Erving was the most dominating presence on the court by far, and second to him was Walter Luckett. Walter scored twenty-eight points that day, second only to Erving's forty-five, while

Frank Oleynick, playing one of his poorer games, managed only two points.

"It was the best game of my life after high school," says Walter. "But Frank didn't have one of his better games. Man, I turned it out. But that Dr. J., he was the greatest. One time he comes down on a fast break and I'm the only player in his way. He stops at the foul line and I thought, good, he's gonna take a jumper. I won't look so bad if he just beats me on a jumper. But what does he do? He slam dunks the ball. From the foul line! What'd I do? I took the ball out of bounds, what else?"

That would be the last time in his career that Walter Luckett would outshine Frank Oleynick in head-to-head or any other competition on a basketball court. It was as if that last effort had drained Walter Luckett, drained him of all that energy he had had to expend over the years in proving to people that he was still Walter Luckett, *the* Walter Luckett. He was drained of his competitive juices in the same way that Muhammad Ali and Joe Frazier were drained of theirs after their third fight in Manila. From then on, whenever Walter and Frank met on a basketball court, it would be a source of continuing and escalating frustration for Walter. For Frank, it would be just the reverse. Eventually Walter's frustration would lead him to challenge Frank to a fight that would become legend in Bridgeport, not for its ferocity but because it was witnessed by so many mutual friends who saw in it final proof of Walter's sad decline. The fight occurred during the summer before their junior year of college, and there are as many versions of its inception and outcome as there were witnesses to it.

Warren Blunt, Walter's best friend: "It all began because Luck was galled at Frank's success, I think. Luck began to get involved in things he shouldn't have. He started bringing out the racial aspect of things, like Frank being white. You could see the fight coming. Frank's attitude was that he was bad too now. He didn't feel Luck was superhuman no more, and so he didn't treat him that way. Before, everyone in Bridgeport used to defer to Walter, and he was used to that. He didn't like the way things were changing. He used to say to me, 'That dude [Frank] be getting on my nerves.' He was jealous, and he knew Frank was a bad dude now, and it was hard for him to admit it, to admit that maybe now Frank was as bad as him. Luck built up this unjustifiable hatred. Now when they hung together it was superficial. Luck would make a joke and Frank would roll his eyes. They were both always trying to throw zingers at each other. They would be in a bar talking shit about some players and Luck would say, 'You know, Lumpkin is bad,' and Frank would roll his eyes and say, 'Sure, Luck, sure.' In Walt's mind, Frank was belittling him. Now Barry, he had no part of this. He's a down dude and he was always trying to keep Frank in line. Barry was always on Frank's case. Frank was a cocky dude just like Luck. Only Frank had more shade to his shit. I remember we were at a party one night and Frank say to me, 'Heh, nigger, whatcha doin' later?' I didn't take no offense cause Frank's black. Walt got upset over it, though. He say to me, 'Why you let him call you nigger?' Then he shakes his head and say, 'Man, that fuckin' Frankie be gettin' on my nerves.' So finally at the University of Bridgeport gym they had it out. Frank elbowed Luck in a pick-up game and Luck got mad. I told Luck to go outside and talk it out like a man. 'Don't be going around with this hatred thing,' I said. 'If you gonna fight, then get it over with.' I say, 'You can talk to Frank. He'll listen.' Walt say Frank don't wanna listen. So Walt challenged him and they went outside and fought. There was a lot of pushin' and swingin' but nobody got hit. Afterwards I felt bad because I had told Walt to do it. I never thought they would. Walt felt bad too. He say, 'That was a stupid thing.' His attitude toward Frank changed after that. So did Frank's toward Luck. Luck changed toward Frank, but Frank changed against Luck. Their signals got crossed. It's funny, but the one the fight hurt the most was Barry. He didn't like it one bit. He told Frank it wasn't right because Frank and Walt were friends."

Barry McLeod: "I had to think Frank's success was part of Walter's problem. It was the first time the two had got together after Frank's sophomore year, when he had got all that ink. We were all playing at the UB gym. Frank's coach, John Waldeyer, and UB Coach Bruce Webster were watching. There were a lot of people there. The fight started because both of them were a lot alike. They had the killer instinct. At least Walter used to have it. Frank had it. They were both cheaters. The fight started because the night before, when they were playing, Walter cheated and tried to get the ball out of bounds. Frank wouldn't let him. He said, 'You can't get those calls anymore, Luckett.' They were calls everyone gave Luckett before. No one would ever think of not giving him those calls. But now Frank challenged him. All the coaches laughed at this. Walter was embarrassed. That night he talked to his man, Blunt, and he told Walt what to do, and the next day it was just a matter of time before Frank and Walt went at it. Walter called Frank outside. He said Frank was trying to belittle him in front of people. He took Frank by surprise. But no one was hurt. I didn't think it was the time or place for it. Shit, friends fighting in the street in front of people! That's not right. When I heard what was happening outside I ran out and separated them."

Walter Luckett: "That fight with Frank at UB started because he told me to shut up in front of a lot of people. There weren't many blacks in the place and I felt Frank was trying to take advantage of me. I thought, this s.o.b. don't respect me, I got to show him. Then the next day, this white kid started talking junk to me. He saw Frank do it so he think he can too. I say, 'You shut up or I'll break your jaw.' Then I said to myself, 'I gotta stop this shit.' Two days later the same thing happens with Frankie. So I say, 'Come outside.' Were there any punches landed? Yeh, mine. I gave him a shot. He didn't get no shots in. But I was wrong. After, I felt bad. It wasn't right. But I had to do it because he was on an ego thing, flying high."

Frank Oleynick: "There's two versions of that fight. Some people say it started because Walt was jealous of me. Some say because I started to show Walt up in front of people. I think it was because of Walt's frustration. But I guess I was very aggressive too. I was proud that I was expressing myself against Walt. If there was any conversing to be done, I wasn't about to back down. But afterwards I felt bad about it. The only good thing was that now it was out in the open. Before, Walt had never confronted me with any derogatory things to my face. I'd always hear it from others. Anyway, it was no real fight, just a wrestling match. Nobody got hit."

Bruce Webster, University of Bridgeport basketball coach: "The fight? Hell, it was no fight, just a lot of pushing and shoving. Frank was the instigator. Walt didn't want to fight. They got into some words in the gym, and the next thing I know they're both outside. I saw twenty kids go follow them, so I went outside too. I saw the whole thing. There was some pushing and shoving and then I broke it up. I think Frank was resentful of Walter from earlier days and was just looking for an excuse to show him up in basketball and outside. Frank wanted that fight, life or death. He would have killed Walter. Walter just didn't want to get hurt. He was backstepping all the way. I sent Frank back into the gym. Outside, Walter was shattered. He was visibly upset in front of his peers. He started to cry. He said to me, 'Coach, all I want to do is play basketball and I can't even do that in my own home town. Everyone takes a potshot at me. Guys like Frankie want to show me up.' Walt was right. Everyone had it in for him. From then on, Frank always seemed to be on top."

There was a sad postscript to that fight at the end of the summer, before the two rivals returned to their respective colleges—an attempt by Walter to get even with Frank for what most felt was his humiliation at the UB gym. It seems that Frank, Walter and Barry were to play together for the Beardsley Terrace coalition league team against a visiting all-black team at the Beardsley Terrace outdoor court. Frank and Barry had played on that all-black coalition team for almost five years. This year the team got a new coach, a black man who did not really know of Frank and Barry's close ties to the Terrace and who suggested that it wasn't right for two white boys to be starting in place of brothers on his team. All the Terrace's black youths like Kenny Sumpter and Don

Clemmons tried to reason with this coach, explaining that Frank at least deserved to start since he was so much better than anyone else the coach might use in his place.

"Frank has never been excluded from the blacks," says Kenny Sumpter. "People in the Terrace go down for him. They sense he's one of them, even when they don't know him. The black thing is to be hip. The hipper you are, the more black you are. Frank is hip. He plays a razzle-dazzle game. Sonny loves him. Luckett, he's the only one in the Terrace who comes up with Frank being white. The coach say he don't want to play Frank ahead of a brother. 'He's just a white boy,' he say. I say, 'But he can play.' I say, 'Luck, you tell him Frank can play.' Luck say, 'He just a white boy.' I had to tell Frank that so he not be deceived by Luck anymore. A lot of people say I shouldn't do that, tell on a brother. But I don't care. I'd do the same for Luck if the situations were reversed. It was a sad situation, you see, 'cause the brother's mind wasn't right at the time."

"Oh, man, I feel embarrassed for him about that story," says Frank. "That was very low. Walt knew I should start."

"I think Walt just say that because he wanted to go with the flow," says Clemmons. "He was trying to be a brother, you know. Walt's always trying to act black. And the funny thing is, Frankie's more black than he is. Even Frankie's game is black. Walter plays a white game. We all say, 'Heh, where'd Walt come from, the suburbs?'"

"I had mixed emotions about the fight," says Barry McLeod. "Naturally a little shield came between us, me and Walt. I was aware of him now when he was around. I learned that night to sit back and watch. But I realize one reason Walt did this was because there was still competition between him and Frank. You see, you got to understand that Walt was not a happy person. He was torn. There was turmoil in his mind. He doesn't trust anybody anymore, he's on the lookout. He thinks people are constantly out to get him. And when people no longer were looking out for him, I mean taking care of him like they always had, it tore him apart. Walter would be a better person without basketball, you see. Maybe we all would. Basketball got us all together, but we might be better friends without it. We're all three so gifted it keeps us apart."

While his cousin's success, and to a lesser extent Walter Luckett's success too, was considerable during their first two years of college, Barry McLeod's career at Centenary College in Shreveport, Louisiana, was not as obvious. In his freshman year he played on his team's junior varsity team and watched the varsity play from the bench. He admits it was a frustrating period for him, the first time in his life that he was not a star. Furthermore, his frustration was heightened because he had to read daily of both his cousin and Walter in their freshman years. Walter's achievements he could live with; it was expected. But this was the first time Barry ever had to take a back seat to his cousin.

"I went to Centenary because I could see with Robert Parish [the team's black seven-foot center] there was a possibility of a national championship," says Barry. "More than personal glory, I liked to win. Frank and Walter were more inclined to seek personal glory. During their years at Seattle and Ohio, their teams were barely over .500. At Centenary during my four years my team was 69 and 14. When I first got to Centenary and wasn't playing as a freshman I was depressed. It was the first time I ever doubted myself. My coach, Larry Little, said to me, 'I know what's bothering you. You see Frank and Walter scoring all those points and you're not even playing. Well, I got four senior guards and they got to play this year. Next year, don't worry, I'll throw you to the wolves.' Then he said, 'Besides, if you and Frank changed places you'd be doing all the scoring and he'd be sitting on the bench here.'

"When I first got there I hated the South. They were so slow. Down south you just throw out schedules. Nobody appreciates time. And the prejudice! Man, nobody should have to live the way the blacks do down south. So many roaches! They're definitely oppressed. That's why, when I come back to Bridgeport, I always go back to the Terrace. Those people got nothing and they still let me into their world. They had every reason to keep me out of the Terrace. Yet they're so real for me, more real than any white people I ever met. They never asked me questions. They just let me play on their court. But yet, after the South, I began to realize the Terrace wasn't so cool anymore and how lucky I was to get out of it. I started to feel relaxed down south. It wasn't confining, like the Terrace. And for the first time in my life I had friends who weren't my cousin, my blood. Guys at Centenary who I lived with. We shared the same bathroom, the same soap. I didn't just grow into them, I had to win them.

"I met people who broadened my world. Like Robert Parish. I consider him my friend. One day after my freshman year I brought him back to Bridgeport to meet Frank. The next day when Frank mentioned a book he thought I should read, I said, 'Yeh, I think I'll get the big man [Parish] to read it too.'" Frank said, 'What the hell, it'll take him two years.' I said, 'You got no call to say that. He's a good man. He's my best friend.' Maybe Frank was jealous or something, I don't know. I know that me and Frank can't go on living like we been. We were starting to grow apart a little even then. I remember one night that summer Frank wanted to go swimming up at Lake Mohegan. At the time my leg was in a cast because I had hurt it during the season, so I couldn't go swimming. He swam out to the center of the lake and then I couldn't see him no more. I started shouting for him. He didn't answer. I started hobbling around the edge of the lake screaming and crying for him, but still there was no answer. I jumped into the water even though I knew I couldn't swim with my leg and all. But still I started after him. I never woulda made it. Then suddenly he comes out of the water and he's laughing. I got so mad I started hitting him. I was crying and screaming at him and hitting him all at the same time. . . . Now we're in college we can't see each other that much anymore. Oh, we're still friends. Frank's my blood, but we got new friends too. For years there was nothing too private for us that we didn't share with one another. About the only thing we never shared was dates. We never got together that much with girls. I can't explain it, really. At Centenary I was always going on dates with my teammates. Sometimes the girls would be black and sometimes white. It didn't make no difference to me.

"Like when I first got there they wanted me to room with the trainer. He was white. I'd never roomed with whites before, except my cousin. I told them I'd room with Leon, a black guy, because he was a player and I was a player. They say, 'You can't do that.' They look at me like I'm strange. Then when I started hanging around with Parish his black friends they useta say, 'You can't come with us. Don't you know there's places for you and there's places for us?' I say, 'That's not the way I was brought up.' One night I took some of my black teammates to a bar downtown and the bartender, who had never checked my I.D., checked theirs. I said, 'You never asked me for mine before.' He say, 'Barry, calm down, I'll see what I can do.' I took my dollar back and we left. Whenever I went to a bar, if they didn't let blacks in I left. Sometimes I'd be with some white friends and they'd say, 'Let's go to a bar,' and I'd say, 'I'll go if it ain't no redneck place.' It's funny, but that was the first time I ever really had much to do with white guys. Most of my friends had been black, and they still were at Centenary. Like I said, I was real close to Robert Parish. We were a lot alike. He was lazy, moody, a real country boy. Frank's more a city boy. Parish and me liked to be off by ourselves a lot. He taught me to how to catfish. I loved it. We'd pick up a six-pack and ride down some dusty dirt road, a real Tobacco Road, and then park somewhere by a stream and just fish for hours. Parish's family lived down an old dirt road across a sewage gully. You had to cross a wooden plank to reach the house. It was a small house, as clean as it could possibly be. Parish's mother was a great lady. She raised five kids. She loved me too. Parish and me got along because we had the same interests—women, beer and basketball. I remember the first time he saw me dribble through my legs. He couldn't believe it. And the way I talked, and dressed. But I'll tell you this, before I left there they was all asking me where

I got this shirt and those slacks, even the white guys. Before I got there, no white and black athletes ever hung together much less roomed together. Now they all be getting together. And why shouldn't they? All college kids are the same. They're all struggling for the same thing."

Barry McLeod became a starting guard at Centenary in his sophomore year. He guided his team to a 21-4 record while averaging almost ten points a game himself. He was the team's point guard, responsible for controlling the tempo of the game, setting up the team's offensive plays and trying to work the ball in to the team's overpowering center, Robert Parish. It was a new role for Barry, who had always been a scoring guard. Now instead of taking twenty-foot jump shots from the head of the key, he concentrated on penetrating to the basket and then passing off to Parish. He sublimated his desire for personal glory for the benefit of the team. It was a role he did not want at first but learned to accept with his team's success. It was a role neither his cousin nor Walter Luckett could ever assume, and yet one they could appreciate in Barry. Walter once said of Barry, "He's the only one of us three who can play with superstars and still be recognized." Even Walter realized that he and Frank thought they had to stack the deck in their favor (inferior teams) in order to excel.

"Frank could never make the transition I had to make in college," says Barry. "I went to a school where I couldn't shoot much. And Walt, I don't think he ever thought of winning. All he thought of was points. I remember when he was being recruited a college coach said to him, 'You can come to my school and run the show.' Walt looked at him and said, 'Run the show! I wanna *be* the show!' I remember when I came home after my sophomore year I went up to the Terrace for a game and Frank and Walter were starting but I wasn't. I felt inferior for the first time. Maybe these guys are better than me, I thought. The crowd was all for Frank and Walt, you know, real front runners. Then I got into the game after about four minutes and hit six long jumpers. The next day the crowd in the Terrace was buzzing how maybe I was better than both Frank and Walter even if I didn't get their ink as a sophomore. I grew up that day. I realized it was just a matter of being in the right place at the right time. I had a good team and so I couldn't shoot that much. I had to get Parish the ball. It would be stupid basketball for me to take twenty-footers with a guy like Parish under the basket."

Barry was able to make this adjustment in his playing style for a number of reasons. Foremost of these was his nature. He was more pliable than either Frank or Walter, and his ego demanded less external satisfaction. He could appreciate the joys of internal delight in a way his cousin or Walter could not. Furthermore, his approach to basketball, his philosophy about the game, was essentially different from Walter and Frank's. For Walter, basketball was a way of bolstering his basic insecurity. Despite his achievements and glory, he was still only the sum of what others had told him. He needed, above all else, external approval, which he got only through basketball. Without it, he feared he would be nothing. Frank's attitude toward basketball was more pragmatic. It was a means of escape from his surroundings to a better life, a not uncommon goal for black ghetto youths.

For Barry McLeod, basketball was a beautiful woman. He was in love with it. "I'm only happy when I'm playing the game," he says. "I play because I love it. It's not to prove anything. When I'm out there, man, it's like I'm free. My friends always get on me, that I'm quiet. But on the court I open up. It's really me. Everything else is on the side. I don't care about nothing else, just running up and down the court, handling the ball, oh man. . . . I make a nice pass, I help somebody out, it's almost a way of life. You pat someone on the ass. Everything's involved in basketball—psychology, you got to relate to them, know when to pass it to them, let them do their thing. You thank 'em. You pick 'em up. It's all natural stuff. It ain't just a game for me, it's a way of life. That's why when I have to stop playing I'll miss it more than my cousin or Walter. It's the only time I'm me.

"It ain't only basketball. I useta love baseball, too. I played a few games for Centenary my first year. I remember one game against Louisiana Tech, they had this big mother pitcher who threw smoke. I sat on the bench watching him for about thirteen innings and I loved him. The way he threw. Then I got in as a pinch hitter with the bases loaded. He goes to 3–0 on me, then he throws a strike. Then I fouled one off—I was right on it, too—and then before the next pitch he walks off the mound toward me and says, 'I'm coming in with it, man.' I loved it. Just loved it. He threw it and I swung, man, and missed it, and it was all beautiful. The next time up maybe I'd hit it three miles."

seven

By the time Frank Oleynick and Walter Luckett finished their junior year both had decided to forego another year of college basketball eligibility and to enter their names in the National Basketball Association's hardship free-agent draft, which would be held in the spring of 1975. Of the three friends, only Barry McLeod chose to remain in school, earn his degree and play his final college season. The reasons for his cousin's and Walter Luckett's choice to "go hardship" were many and varied. Some were the same for both players and some were particular to each one.

When Frank Oleynick finished his junior season at the University of Seattle he was already a virtual legend in the city. He held almost all the school's individual scoring records, had come in fourth in a newspaper survey to pick the Seattle "Man of the Year" and would, within the next eighteen months, be chosen one of the ten best basketball players ever to play in the West Coast Athletic Conference. (The best player ever to play in that conference was deemed to be Bill Russell, the former Boston Celtic great, who was then head coach and general manager of the NBA Seattle Supersonics.) For Frank Oleynick there were few worlds left to conquer in college basketball. He had been a number of second- and third-team All-American choices and had been consistently in the top ten in scoring in the nation during his sophomore and junior seasons, averaging twenty-seven points a game. Furthermore, it had proved increasingly difficult for him to sustain that average during his junior year for a number of reasons. As an established scorer he was now being double- and triple-teamed by opposing defenses, whereas as an unknown sophomore he was free to score off only one defender. Also, since the team had lost many of its better players prior to his junior year, he was forced to shoulder a greater burden for its success than before. "He was the 'Magic Man,' " says Dave Bike, the assistant coach. "The year before he had won all those games at the buzzer, and now as a junior he felt he had to take all those last-second shots. Only this year they weren't going in and we would lose. We didn't surround him with real good players in his junior year, and the prospects weren't much better for his senior year. He was always being double-teamed at least, and he began to get down on his teammates and his coach. I told him if he didn't like it he could go back to Bridgeport and play for a factory team."

This realization, that he would have to play even better as a senior merely to duplicate his sophomore and junior achievements, was just one of the reasons that persuaded Frank Oleynick it would be to his advantage to go hardship in his junior year. Also, he could see that a merger between the National and the American Basketball Association loomed on the horizon, and with it would be a decrease in his bargaining power. With two leagues bidding for his services, he felt he could command much more money than with only one. For the first time in his life money had become important to him. With it he could improve his family's circumstances. He could move them out of the Terrace area and into the suburbs. And Frank was not averse to improving his own situation either. He had never thought much about money so long as his prospects of having it were dim, but he had always appreciated fine things, even in his early teens. "When I was fifteen," he says, "I saw an ad in a magazine that showed a beautiful sorta English mansion with a circular driveway. There was a beautiful blonde woman standing beside a car, a Mercedes-Benz. I remember thinking how I'd like to be in that picture."

Frank felt his chance of getting enough money to buy that car and have that girl were excellent in his junior year. First of all, he was so popular in Seattle that it would be to the city's professional team's advantage to draft him highly. "When Frank played for Seattle U. opposite the Sonics," says Bruce Webster, "he outdrew them. Russell *had* to draft him. The media pressured him to do so. Frank was a hero there." Furthermore, whenever Frank played in pickup games against Sonics' stars such as Slick Watts or Freddy Brown, he more than held his own. "Frank destroyed Slick Watts," says Mark Kaufman, the college's radio broadcaster. "Slick didn't even show up anymore when he knew Frank was gonna be around."

And finally, Frank Oleynick was confident he would receive a lot of money in the NBA draft because he knew Bill Russell liked him both as a person and a player. Russell had seen Frank play in college only once, against his own alma mater, the University of San Francisco. Frank had scored thirty points that night and Russell was impressed. He was particularly impressed by

Frank's bruising, hard-nosed style of play and by his black game. No matter what Russell's own prejudices were, and they were rumored to be bitter, as a general manager he appreciated the fact that a white man playing a black game in the NBA was just what Seattle, or any NBA team, needed. It was this irony, that Frank was white and played a black game, that largely determined how high the bidding would go for his services. Most of the players in the NBA are black. Most of the fans who pay money for tickets to NBA games are white. Those fans admire the talent of the blacks, but nonetheless they look eagerly for an occasional "white hope" in their home team's lineup.

In his junior year a number of sports agents contacted Frank Oleynick and asked to handle his future contract negotiations. Frank, an astute judge of human nature despite his age, chose Jerry Kapstein, a boyish-looking New Englander who would soon build a reputation for handling multimillion-dollar contracts for baseball players. At the time he agreed to handle Frank's affairs, Kapstein had no basketball players under his wing. He immediately entered into negotiations with Bill Russell even before the 1975 draft to test the waters for his client. "We told Russell what we wanted," says Kapstein "and Russell looked Frank right in the eye and told him he couldn't name a figure now but that in light of what Frank was seeking, he still wanted to draft him first in the first round." It was Russell's way of telling Frank that he would pay pretty much what he was asking, provided, of course, Frank was still available when Seattle's pick came around. Seattle picked twelfth that year. Russell told Frank that not one guard after the eighth pick would get more money than him. He was true to his word. When Seattle drafted Frank twelfth, their first-round pick, they offered him a five-year, $700,000 package deal that included a number of incentive bonuses and a guarantee of about $125,000 per year for the first two years of the contract. Seattle would have to pick up Frank's option for the last three years of that contract for him to continue to receive that salary.

After Frank officially signed his Sonics contract, Bill Russell himself flew Frank's entire family out to Seattle and put them up in an expensive downtown hotel. It was a gesture that impressed Frank. "Russell's a helluva man. I admire him more than anyone I've ever met," Frank said at the time. Mr. Oleynick was impressed too, but less with Russell the man than with his life-style. "Mr. Russell has a million-dollar house," says Mr. Oleynick, not without bitterness. "He gets a salary of $250,000 a year. He owns part of the franchise. He has a shirt factory that puts pictures of basketball players on the shirts. He's a multimillionaire. He has a bar and a TV in his car, in one of his cars. He has four: a Maserati or something, a Mercedes-Benz, a Cadillac and a Rolls Royce. He had a four-car garage and only three cars, so he had to go out and get another. He has a deal with a Mercedes-Benz dealership in Los Angeles, and he helped Frank get his car there. I told Frank I didn't think it was such a good idea buying a $20,000 car, but he didn't listen."

The first thing Frank bought with his newfound wealth was a blue Mercedes-Benz 450 SE. After a few weeks he traded it in for a larger chocolate colored 450 SEL. "The SE was a little cramped," he says. Dave Bike says, "The joke around Seattle was that Frank's SE needed an oil change so he bought a new one." Adds

Bruce Webster, "I told him that car would come back to haunt him. Hell, here's a kid who never had a thing and now he's got a $22,000 car!"

If Frank seemed too willing to gratify himself with his money, he was even more willing to do the same for his parents and friends. First he donated $4000 to Seattle University. Then he bought his family a $50,000 house outside Stratford, Connecticut, a pleasant suburb of Bridgeport. He also bought his father a new car and convinced him, at the age of fifty, to retire from his job. Frank then took over the burden of supporting his family to the tune of about $1000 a month. Nor did he forget his boyhood friends. He flew Barry McLeod and Dennis McLaughlin out to Las Vegas to celebrate his good fortune, and from that moment on he took it upon himself to support all of his friends whenever they were in his company. There was even a rumor going around Bridgeport that he had showed his appreciation to his cousin by buying him a car. "It wasn't true," says Barry. "If he had I woulda taken it. Why not? I woulda done the same thing for him if the situations were reversed."

Don Clemmons summed up the attitude of all Frank's friends back in Bridgeport when he said, "When Frank made it, it was like all of us made it. When he played against Earl Monroe, it was like we were playing against The Pearl. We shared in everything he did. We were so proud of him. When he played in a Rucker game after he signed, some black dudes were saying, 'Where's the white dude who got $700,000? That little white dude can't be him.' And Frank killed them that day. It was like we was playing. And why not? Frank was luckier than us, that's all. I had dreams, too. To be elite. We all coulda been there but for one reason or another."

"I didn't envy my cousin," says Barry. "But I wondered why him? Why not me? We used to sleep in the same bed together. Before we went to sleep we kneeled down and prayed. We prayed for the same things. Why did they come to him? Maybe he was just in the right place at the right time, that's all."

Many of Walter Luckett's reasons for going hardship in his junior year were similar to Frank's and some were unique to Walter. However, there were many elements in Walter's situation that argued convincingly for his not taking such a step.

Like Frank, Walter justifiably feared an impending NBA-ABA merger, which would seriously cut into his bargaining power. He also was destined to play for a mediocre team in his senior year, which would force him to work harder at merely duplicating his sophomore and junior year achievements (twenty-three and twenty-five points per game, respectively). Furthermore, like Frank, Walter Luckett wanted to advance his family's social status with the money he thought he would receive on being drafted. Here there was a subtle difference, however, between the aims of the two friends and rivals. Whereas Frank felt his family needed that money desperately to save it from despair, Walter merely wanted to add to his family's creature comforts and improve their social position. Without that money Walter's family would survive. His father had always landed on his feet, no matter how severe a setback he suffered. Frank's family was deteriorating, however, and on his shoulders fell the responsibility of saving it. He carried his family in a way that Walter was carried by his. Walter wanted to show his appreciation for what his family had given him while Frank wanted to support his family in a way they had been unable to support him.

"I want to make it for my family," says Walter. "We're still young. I want us to come together, enjoy our youth, get away from it all. You know, the ghetto, confusion. My brothers, they have to carry knives to protect themselves. I want to get them away from that, out into the suburbs. And my father, too. No one knows how much he wants me to make it. I want to pay him back. I have a goal. To get married, be a family man. To have money so I won't have to work. I'll have people work for me. Maybe Frankie will come in and do P.R. for me. And I want to add to the family name, have five boys and one girl. I want the Luckett name to expand. I hope when I'm sixty my kids will be successful so I can visit them all over the country. I want to be at a dinner table with all my kids around me. The top honcho. Ha! That's a trip. You see, kids make you feel good. They're your blood. All you. But different, too."

Walter's desire to start a family and his basic loneliness at Athens were the primary considerations in his decision to get married early in his junior year. With that marriage came new obligations that caused him to worry considerably about money. "For the first time in his life," says George Fasolo, "money was a necessity for him. Before, his basketball had always brought him anything he needed for himself, but now he had new obligations. A wife. A car. An apartment. He felt pressure for the first time. He became very money conscious."

The girl Walter married was Valita Holley, a beautiful black co-ed from Brown University in Rhode Island. She was intelligent and self-secure, probably more so than her new husband, which made for an odd match.

Although she was enamored of Walter Luckett, the basketball hero, he was even more enamored of her, of her beauty and brightness. "Walter was always scared of losing Valita," says Don Clemmons. "She was off on her own at Brown, you know. Walt didn't like that. He was very insecure about her."

"I had all the girls I wanted at Ohio U.," says Walter, "but they never meant anything to me. They only wanted me because I was Walter Luckett. I had a complex about that. I was awful lonesome there. Finally I called Valita and said, 'Come on down here, there ain't nobody real here.'"

The reasons against Walter's going hardship were significant. He was not a legend in Athens as Frank was in Seattle. Although Walter had experienced what most athletes would consider a successful college career, those people who had seen him play in high school agreed he had never fulfilled his earlier potential. In fact, old friends like Kenny Sumpter would claim that Walter's talent had atrophied. If he remained in school for his senior year he might yet exhibit the kind of talent he once had. Furthermore, there was no NBA team in Athens (as there was in Seattle) whose local press was clamoring for Walter to play for his college town's pro team. In fact, there were no NBA teams as anxious to sign Walter in his junior year as there were to sign Frank. And finally, Walter was black and played a white game. This had always been to his advantage in his youth, when whites rallied around him. But now, in the cold financial world of professional sport, it would work to his disadvantage. Most NBA business managers felt that a black player playing a white game was more a liability than an asset at the ticket office, preferring to sign a white player playing such a game. And there were plenty of those around, all playing a similar game to Walter's. If it came down to choosing between Walter and a white player of comparable ability, the white player would almost assuredly get the nod.

Walter understood these arguments, but they did not deter him for a number of reasons. In the final analysis, the deciding factor was that he was still competing with Frank Oleynick.

"Frank and I been competing all our lives," says Walter. "When I made my decision to go hardship I based it on Frankie's. I thought I was better than him at the time. Still, I wasn't sure I'd get as much money because I was black and he was white. It wasn't a racist thing, really, it was just black players are a dime a dozen in the NBA. White players like Frankie, especially ones who play a black game, are at a premium."

Don Clemmons says of his friends, "To this day they're still rivals. They get along okay, but still in the back of Luck's mind, he and Frankie are rivals. During the hardship draft Luck would call Frankie in Seattle and say, 'What you gonna do?' Frankie told him. That convinced Walt he had to go hardship too, and ask for more money than Frankie. I told Luck at the time not to worry about how much Frankie got. He say, 'Shut up! You crazy!' I say, 'But you don't realize, Frankie's in the right place at the right time. He's in a city with a franchise.' I tried to calm Luck down, but he wouldn't listen. One thing I never did come out and tell him was that Frankie did a lot more than he had in college."

Once Walter's decision to go hardship was made known in the press, scores of players' agents descended on the Ohio U. campus seeking to represent him, just as they had done for Frank Oleynick. Unlike Frank, however, Walter did not pick one single agent he felt could do the best for him. He let two and three agents think they were negotiating for him, under the premise that there was safety in numbers. Walter felt the agents would be competing among themselves to get him the best contract. The opposite resulted, however. Once the Detroit Pistons had drafted Walter as their first pick in the second round (Detroit had no first-round pick and so Walter was the twenty-seventh player drafted that year, while Frank Oleynick was the twelfth draftee), they were besieged by agents all claiming to represent Walter Luckett. The Piston general manager, Oscar Feldman, began to see Walter Luckett as a potential headache to his organization even before he had signed him to a contract.

This attitude toward Walter was further solidified when Walter finally did settle on one agent to do his negotiating. That agent was Arnie Jacobs, a born-and-bred New Yorker still in his twenties. He was one of the breed particular to New York City whose lives are played out in the shadows of Madison Square Garden. They frequent any and every sporting event in the Garden, are enamored of the athletes, never athletic themselves, and calculate ways to join their golden company. At the time Arnie Jacobs met Walter Luckett in 1974, he worked for Walt Frazier Enterprises, which was run by Irwin Weiner, an athletes' agent. Walt Frazier once described Arnie Jacobs as nothing more than a "bus driver" for his organization. Still, it was an organization that impressed Walter Luckett, one he wanted to be part of. Walter remembers being chauffeured about New York City by Walt Frazier and his bodyguard, "Sweet"

Baker, in Frazier's Rolls Royce. They went to a number of New York City nightclubs, where Frazier was greeted extravagantly by his fans, most of whom seemed, to Walter, to be stylish blonde women. Walter was impressed by such a life, yet he held back from giving Walt Frazier Enterprises exclusive rights to negotiate his contract. "I didn't want to be a small fish in a big pond," says Walter. After all, he could never in his wildest dreams surpass Frazier's eminence in his own company, and so Walter looked around for a smaller organization where he would be the feature attraction. This was where Arnie Jacobs came in. He told Walter he would be willing to leave Walt Frazier Enterprises and start his own agency if Walter would sign on with him. He promised Walter a percentage of the business and hinted that, who knows, it might someday be known as Walt Luckett Enterprises.

"I went with Arnie because I liked him better than Irwin Weiner," says Walter. "I judge people by their character. And Arnie said I was gonna be his number one man. I dug that. He put all his emphasis on me."

Warren Blunt, Walt's closest friend and adviser, was not so taken with Jacobs: "After I met Jacobs I says to Walt, 'You sure this guy on the level? Has he got your best interests at heart?' Walt say, 'Yeh, he cool.' As time went on we saw that Jacobs wasn't worth shit. Walt would say to him, 'Arnie, we gonna go to Detroit and sign a contract and have our picture taken. Me and you. Smiling, holding up this big check for one million dollars. Don't you worry, you take care of me and I'll take care of you.' The problem was that Arnie should have assumed a role over Walt, but he was so impressed with Walt he let Walt tell him what to do, how much to ask for. I say, 'Walt, you serious? A million?' Walt say stupid things like 'Shit, I ain't worth just no $30,000. John Williamson only got $17,000 his first year.' I got mad and say, 'Yeh, but the man is bad. He's in the NBA. He's got potential. He's gonna get over. He'll play for $17,000 this year but next year he'll get over.' Walt say, 'Shit, $17,000 ain't nothing to me.' I say, 'You ain't never had nothing in your life and you talking that $17,000 ain't nothing to you. You a crazy nigger.' But his mind was blown by Jacobs. He built Walt up to think he was another 'Clyde.' And that's just what Walt wanted to believe."

Walter Luckett and Arnie Jacobs' negotiations with the Detroit Pistons were a disaster from the very first moment they walked into a room to bargain with acting General Manager Oscar Feldman.

"Before Ray Scott [the Detroit coach] drafted me," says Walter, "he called me on the phone in Athens and told me if I was still around when they got their pick, he'd draft me. I asked what figures he was thinking of. He said in the $70,000 range and we'll work up from there. I said that was fine with me. Then when we [Walt, Arnie Jacobs and Walt's wife] walked into that negotiating meeting with Oscar Feldman and Ray Scott, Feldman said the coach had no right talking those figures without his approval. Then he offered me $130,000 for three years, but not with a no-cut contract. Arnie Jacobs turns around and asks for $175,000 a year for five years with bonuses. Yep, that's what he asked for. Me? I didn't ask for it, ha, ha! Then Oscar Feldman says, 'Well, it looks like we're in different ballparks.' Arnie says, 'We sure are. We're in such different ballparks that we're leaving. You can play this game by yourselves. I already got a $300,000 offer for Walter from Indiana of the ABA.' I don't think that was true, really. Then my wife says,

'Walt, why don't you prove yourself for a year if they don't think you're as good as you are.' Jacobs cut her off even while Oscar Feldman was agreeing with my wife. Then Arnie started breaking down their players and telling Ray Scott what was wrong with each one. I don't think they appreciated that. There was a little flare-up and we left. Scott was pissed off at my agent, and why wouldn't he be? I was very disillusioned with the whole bargaining thing. I think Jacobs blew it. Maybe he meant well, but he was a little hasty. Then while we continued to negotiate over the summer he advised me not to go to Detroit's rookie camp, and that hurt me."

At the time these negotiations were taking place, the Detroit front office was in a period of transition. Ed Coyle, the team's general manager, was about to step down from that position and be replaced by Oscar Feldman, an attorney, who for all intents and purposes already had assumed the team's general manager's role.

Oscar Feldman, a precise little man in his fifties, has neatly clipped gray hair and the aura of one who has controlled the purse strings all his life, ever since he got his first paper route. He says of those negotiations, "I think Walter's best spokesman at that meeting was his wife. She was very intelligent. I was impressed with her reasoning and the questions she asked. Jacobs, on the other hand, kept comparing Walter to Jerry West and Oscar Robertson. He wanted a six-digit bonus, and a salary to boot of six digits. We told him he hadn't done his homework as to what a second-round draft choice like Walter gets. We offered Walter, over a three-year period, a sum in the low to medium five-digit figure per year, with a bonus in the low four-digit area. Jacobs was astounded. There was no opportunity for any true negotiations, so they went back east. If Ray Scott had made Walt the offer over the phone that Walt said he did, then he did so without our approval. There was no doubt in my mind what parameters we were going to offer. As a player there was a question of Walt's defensive ability, and there was unanimity of opinion on this assessment. Also, he could shoot over people, we knew, but could he go around them?"

After Jacobs broke off negotiations with Detroit he pursued an ABA team, Memphis, that had drafted Walter in the ABA's third round. But before long that team folded, while the two teams that were to replace it, Baltimore and Hartford, never materialized. Hartford, says Walter, would have been ideal for him. "With my name in Connecticut we woulda drawn thousands," he says. Walter was operating under an illusion that he could still capitalize on his high school fame in his home state. Even during the summer, while he was waiting out his negotiations with Detroit and the ABA teams, he wandered around the city as if glory and its rewards were due him, not from his recent achievements but from those of the past. For instance, he asked his old mentor, George Fasolo, for a job, and then when he was hired as an instructor in Fasolo's youth basketball camp, he treated the job cavalierly.

"The camp started promptly at 9 A.M. every morning," says Fasolo. "Walter was fifteen minutes late the first day. Then he left early. He was late a lot that first week. I told him he was being paid and that I wanted him to be on time. He gave me some lip. I told him to take his gear and screw. He said I couldn't do that because I owed him. I threatened to slap his head off his shoulders if he didn't get outta my sight in a hurry. Fifteen minutes after he left I got a call from his mother. 'What did you do to my Walter?' she says. 'People been using him all his life. You're the one person he trusted and now you turned on him. You owe him an apology.' I told her she got it all wrong. Walter owed me an apology."

After the demise of their ABA negotiations, Walter and Jacobs turned back to Detroit. But now they had lost even the slim bargaining edge they had held when Walter was drafted. At that time Detroit desperately needed a shooting guard, but over the long summer of Walter's negotiations, Detroit picked up two such guards on trades, Kevin Porter and Archie Clark, and Walter was no longer even as desirable as he had been. Furthermore, he had missed the team's rookie camp held during the summer, at which he might have impressed Detroit enough to convince them to increase their offer—as a number of other rookie guards who attended had favorably impressed both Scott and Feldman. With nowhere to turn and the season about to get underway, Walter and Jacobs accepted Oscar Feldman's original offer. Walter was given a $7500 bonus and a three-year contract calling for $43,000, $47,000 and $53,000 per year. Unlike Frank Oleynick's contract, however, Walter's guaranteed him nothing but that modest bonus until he proved his worth.

"To tell you the truth," says Oscar Feldman, "I was so upset over those negotiations, they had taken so long, that I was ready to throw in the towel. But Ray Scott said he wanted Walter in camp anyway. I wouldn't have signed him if I wasn't so new to my position. In retrospect, I would have been firmer with Scott."

After Walter finally did sign he became bitter and blamed Arnie Jacobs for his problems. "Shit, I listen to all these suckers feeding me bullshit and believed them," he said. "Hell, I never had nothing in my life and here I am turning my nose up at $43,000 a year. Ha! Ain't that a bitch."

Although Warren Blunt criticized the way Jacobs handled the negotiations ("I shoulda been Walter's agent," he says), he still did not believe that all the blame for what resulted should fall on Jacobs' shoulders. He felt Walter had received so many rewards so soon in his youth that he had come to see them as his due, even when he no longer was producing the results to warrant them. "Walt wasn't thinking right," he says. "I told him he gotta crawl before he walks. I say, 'Don't worry about the money, 'cause if you're bad they gotta pay you.' But he wasn't thinking about his ability. He wasn't thinking that money should be secondary to his talent. And then too, he was obsessed with getting more than Frankie. When things backfired he was like a kid who didn't get his toy. He wanted to talk about blame, and I say, 'It comes right down to you, fella. You picked your agent, you told him what to ask for and you are to blame.' It's funny. It takes a complicated person to make things easy. Any fool can make simple things complicated. Frank, for instance, is a complicated dude, but he's simple too. Like, he looks into the future, not always looking back at the past. I dig where the dude's coming from. . . . You know, I was as good as both of them when I was young. I feel to this day I shoulda been Walter. I shoulda had his success. But I don't envy him. Still, I shoulda been bad, badder than him. I wonder about it sometimes. But he's supposed to be there, I guess. He's 6-3. I stopped growing too soon. He's got the talent. If he makes it, I'll be a part of it too."

When Walter Luckett arrived in Detroit late in the

summer of 1975 for the Pistons' preseason training camp, he pulled up in front of Cobo Hall in a new aqua-and-white Cadillac Coup de Ville. This flamboyant entrance did not sit well with the Pistons' management, nor with their veteran players, who felt Walter's ostentatious display was a bit premature for a rookie who had yet to even make the team. Will Robinson, a Piston scout, said his first impression of Walter Luckett was that he was "a fucking head case." Adds Robinson, "He pulls up in this Cadillac and then proceeds to act like a fucking superstar. Within one week nobody on the team could stand him. He had this idea that basketball couldn't get along without Walter Luckett, but it could. Remember 'Fly' Williams and Larry Fogel? They're not in this league anymore. The word got around."

One of Walter's problems was that he was still thinking and acting like the Walter Luckett of old, the fifty-point scorer whose picture had adorned the cover of *Sports Illustrated*. However, he had not played like that man in three years. His troubles now were further aggravated by his not having gone to the team's rookie camp, a slight the team's players and management felt was Walter's way of saying he was too good to be grouped with the other rookies. Also, he had sprained his ankle during the summer and was unable to work out heavily. He had gained almost twenty pounds and was more out of shape than any player in camp. Walter's haughty attitude, which did not fit either his status or ability, caused him to fall immediately into disfavor with Ray Scott and his players. They took to harassing Walter, a form of college hazing they reserved for all rookies but applied to Walter with what he took to be excessive zeal. Walter took exception to the hazing because, for one thing, he thought he was above it (after all, he *was* Walter Luckett) and, for another, because of his extreme sensitivity. He felt this was being unfairly administered to him over all the other rookies. And he was right. The Detroit veterans always reserved the severest hazing for the team's top rookie pick. It was, in a way, a compliment to him. Also, once the veterans saw how sensitive Walter was, they increased their antics. If he had handled it more tactfully, they probably would have dropped it.

Over in the Seattle Supersonics' training camp Frank Oleynick was undergoing the same type of thing. It barely affected him. Frank was intelligent enough to circumvent it by merely avoiding contact with his team's veterans whenever he could. When confronted by their hazing he acquiesced to their wishes. And when he felt their demands were too demeaning, he simply refused to comply. Once when Spencer Heywood, then a Seattle star, asked him to do something he felt was an affront to his dignity, Frank told Heywood off. Frank could afford this luxury because he exuded the kind of toughness that backed up his belligerent words, and because he had a no-cut contract, a luxury Walter did not have.

"They made a fool out of me," says Walter. "I shed tears. I'm a grown man and I actually cried. I don't like waiting on no one. They called me 'boy' 100 times a day. They made me drink pitcher after pitcher of beer until I vomited. It was a horrible experience. I hated everybody there—Lanier, George Trapp, Curtis Rowe, Ray Scott. The shit they gave me was ridiculous. Low class, very low class. I hated the whole organization. Can you imagine Bill Bradley or Walt Frazier of the Knicks doing anything like that? Man, I wanted to do violence to people. One night George Trapp grabbed my butt. We almost got into it over that. They tried to make me feel I was nothing as a person. It screwed up my mind. It was so degrading I lost my confidence on the court. I couldn't sleep. They wouldn't let me. They'd call me up at all hours of the night and make me go on errands for them. Then I had to be on the court at 6 A.M., two hours before the veterans. Lanier made me run his drills for him. I was worn down and couldn't perform. My shit was sloppy, I admit it. And they *were* harder on me. Maybe it was because I was too sensitive. I took it harder than the others. But it's a lie I had a bad attitude. I wanted to be a part of that team, but the vets had it in for me because I had held out during the summer. They made my attitude what it was. I do have this problem about being sensitive. My face shows it. I hang my head. More than a few times I went into the locker room and cried. They got on me about my car, but I bought that with some money I had saved up in college. Shit, their measly $7500 bonus couldn't buy that car. Besides, it was none of their business what I did with my money."

Walter's disillusionment with his first pro basketball training camp did not lie solely with the treatment accorded him. He was also disillusioned by his teammates' behavior off the court, even those who were not particularly hard on him.

"Howard Porter was okay to me," says Walter. "He's a very intellectual guy. He sued the NCAA for a million dollars! Imagine! Everyone at Detroit was afraid of him. He'd stop running wind sprints and Ray Scott wouldn't do nothing about it. Porter would say, 'Fuck it. Fire me.' And they wouldn't. I'm a dedicated athlete, and it turned me off to see someone not dedicated like me and rolling in money. But that's life. You can't question it.

Maybe I was riding too high and the Lord wanted to open my eyes."

Walter's disillusionment with his teammates, coaches and surroundings affected his play during the camp. He claims he looked "no better, no worse" than any of the other rookies, but most of the Detroit people who saw him during that period claim he looked absolutely inept. Even his once vaunted shooting suffered. In fact, Walter looked so bad that Ray Scott rarely used him in the team's preseason games, except for one game held in the New Haven Coliseum against the New York Knicks. It was here, only a year earlier, that Walter had had his best game since high school against a team of pros led by Julius Erving. Most of his friends from Bridgeport journeyed to New Haven to watch Walter play for the first time as a pro. One of those friends was Don Clemmons.

"Before the game, while Detroit was warming up, we all went down to the court to see Luck," says Clemmons. "It was funny, you know, he acted like he was ashamed of us. Like he didn't want to slap five. He gave me five, but he looked around like he was embarrassed. People were looking at him and he was trying to be cool. Later, when Frank came into Madison Square Garden with the Sonics, we all went to that game too. Sumpter had $50 he'd saved up and he was gonna treat us all to tickets. He said he'd spend it all just to see Frankie. When we got to the Garden I said, 'Heh, just for the hell of it let's check the ticket counter.' Sure enough, Frankie had left us tickets. We walked right into the Garden and down to the floor where the Sonics were warming up. When Frankie sees us he comes over and starts slapping five. A lot of people were looking at us, you know, five black guys, slapping five with this little white dude on the Sonics. Frankie didn't even notice them. After the game he got permission from Russell to come back to Bridgeport with us, and we spent the whole night drinking wine in the Terrace. He loves me, Frankie. I believe Luck loves me, too, but it's just when the brother gets around people he don't want to show what he feels. But the two be different, you know. After one of Frankie's games in New York, we all went to this New York nightclub, Leviticus, where the athletes hang. Frankie didn't dig it and we left right away for the Port. Walter likes going into New York City to those places. He goes with his white friends."

Walter had one of the worst games of his career that night in New Haven. He missed eight shots without making one, and more than once failed even to hit the rim with a shot. At one point he drove toward the basket, had his shot blocked and fell to the floor, a gesture Don Clemmons claims was feigned. "The action moved up the other end of the court," says Clemmons, "but Walter stayed there on the floor, crying to the referee." Clemmons and the rest of Walter's friends were shocked at such a display and also disappointed by how poorly Walter played in general. They wondered what had happened to the Walter Luckett they had once known.

A few days after that New Haven game, back in Detroit, Walter Luckett was released by the Pistons barely two weeks after their training camp had opened. Recalling that moment, he says, "After the New Haven game Scott was quoted in the Bridgeport paper saying that I was overweight and out of shape. He didn't use me at all in the next game, and I knew something was up. When he called me up to cut me, he said I didn't fit into their plans. He said the acquisition of Archie Clark hurt my chances. I didn't say nothin'. I went back to the hotel, packed my bags, picked up my wife at the airport (she had just flown in that night) and we turned around and drove back to Bridgeport. Before we did, though, I got a call from Oscar Feldman. He say that he really wanted me to make the club but that it was Ray's decision to cut me. Then he say I was a fine gentleman, and he hopes I'm not mad at him. I said I appreciated his kind words but I didn't have anything to say. I hung up . . . I was thinking, you motherfucker, let me get my hands on your neck, you sonuvabitch. If I had a gun I woulda shot them both. Ray Scott was tellin' me my career was *over!* Like I wasn't shit! None of 'em didn't give me no respect! Those fucking guys didn't think I could play the game! *I played this fucking game all my life!* They thought I was a con! A *clown!* I ain't no clown. They fucked up my mind, man. But still, I got one thing in my favor. The club quit me, I never quit them. I never quit nothing in my life."

When Walter returned to Bridgeport he did not show his face around the city for weeks. Then, finally, he ventured out to visit George Fasolo. It was Fasolo who had told him not to go hardship in his junior year but to remain in school and at least get his college degree. He told Fasolo that he should have heeded those words. "There isn't a day I wake up and look in the mirror that I don't wish I'd listened to you," Walter said. Then, for the second time that summer, Walter asked Fasolo for a job. Fasolo got him one as a recreation adviser in the P. T. Barnum Housing Project. "Then I told him to get rid of that Caddy and get a station wagon," says Fasolo. "But he didn't listen. . . . One day I went to P. T. and saw where he worked. I wanted to throw up. All his potential!"

It is two years after Walter Luckett had been cut by the Detroit Pistons. Arnie Jacobs, his former agent, and a companion sit at the bar in the lobby of the Roosevelt Hotel in New York City.

Arnie Jacobs now lives in Yonkers with his brother, Danny, an accountant. This night Arnie is wearing a brown doubleknit suit with white piping outlining the lapels, the kind of suit one sees often in the Midwest. He is also wearing a tan shirt and a brown tie, the shorter end of which is tucked inside his shirt. His shoes are black and plain, and his socks are bright orange. His friend, who is skinny and small in comparison to Jacob's soft chubbiness, is floating inside a too-large aquamarine double-breasted suit.

Arnie Jacobs introduces his companion as "Howie, my business associate." Then he says they are on their way to Madison Square Garden to catch a college basketball doubleheader. "There might be some players there I can get into the Italian Basketball League," he adds. "I'm still in the athletic management business—I place players in Europe—but I don't involve myself in the negotiating aspect anymore. I don't like it. My affairs with Walter hurt me very much. I thought I could at least get him into the pros. I mean, his picture was on the cover of *Sports Illustrated!* When I signed him up as my first client, I had friends coming out of the woodwork telling me I had signed the next Walt Frazier. But I hadn't seen him play at that point. I just knew what people told me. And what he told me.

"Walter did a great selling job on me. He told me

that Frank Oleynick got $700,000 and that he was better than Frank. He had to get more money than Frank, he said. Walter was very hurt that Frank was picked ahead of him in the draft. Two days before the draft I talked to Oscar Feldman and I could see that Detroit wasn't that interested in Walter, so I advised him to take his name off the hardship draft. But he wouldn't. I think his father pressured him to keep it on. Then, during the negotiations, Detroit cut him up, and it was obvious to me they didn't think highly of him. I also had the problem that Walter had let other people negotiate for him while I was. One of these agents, a car dealer from Athens, was in collusion with Detroit to undermine my efforts. Detroit tried to alienate me in favor of him, because he had made a prearranged deal with them. I warned him to leave Walter alone, but Mr. Luckett said, 'We got to stay on the good side of him because he's fixin' Walter's car.'

"Oh, I admit I made some mistakes too. Like bringing Walt's wife along. She kept agreeing with Oscar Feldman. I also made a mistake asking for a million dollars. That *was* a mistake. But I was just negotiating! I would have taken anything as long as it was a no-cut contract. I wanted to get Walter into the NBA in the worst way. He was my first client. I was gonna form a business around him. Making money was not my main concern. . . . Then, after they signed him, they cut him so quick. I couldn't understand it. He was their number one pick. Why couldn't they look him over a little longer? It would only cost them meals and hotel expenses. Now I think the only reason they took him to New Haven for the exhibition game with the Knicks was to draw some Connecticut fans to see him so they could recoup part of their bonus expenditure. After Walter was cut I called every NBA and ABA team, and no one wanted even to take a look at him. They said it was too late in training. Their rosters were already set. Finally I told Walter that maybe it was me. Maybe he should get another agent.

"A year later—I hadn't seen Walter now—I pick up a Cleveland paper and see where Walter says how I screwed him. Jeez, I invested several thousand dollars in him and I only got back $800 from his bonus! I sent him $100 a week! I sent him airplane tickets! He ruined the transmission in my car! He ran up over $1200 in telephone bills on me! His brothers ate me outta house and home! His father drank all of my liquor! I was a nervous wreck! I bought Walter a complete wardrobe so he could go to Detroit for the negotiations and look sharp. I'm still paying off my investment in Walter Luckett. He was my man. I loved him. I was gonna die with him, you know what I mean. He killed me. It never occurred to me he would get cut. He really fooled me. He looks like a superstar. He talks like one too, you know. For a black guy, he's so clean-cut. He fools you. But he doesn't have that mental toughness. He seemed to have a lot of confidence off the court. He was the king. But that was only on the surface. He didn't play like no Walter Luckett. He didn't play like a guy who had to make the team. I saw him play in New Haven and I was shocked. He didn't look like a pro. Yet I always treated him like a professional. That was another mistake. I should have treated him like a kid. I didn't tell him to stay in shape over the summer because I assumed he would. What I should have done was go out and run with him.

"I made another mistake too. I couldn't read into the

fact that Walter was a weak person. He'd call me every night at 3 A.M. to be reassured. He'd say, 'Everything's gonna be all right, isn't it, Arnie?' I really think he needs a psychiatrist. He was always crying about something. People drove him to it, sure, but it was his own fault. He let them. He'd rather be pretty than tough. Maybe he had talent once, but no more. Too many people spoiled him. His family. His father. I feel bad for the old man. Everything was Butchy, Butchy, Butchy. His dream. The other kids suffered for it.

"Where does Walter Luckett go from here? I don't know. I saw him recently and he wouldn't shake my hand. Then one night, December 29, 1976, he calls me up and asks me for money. Just like that! He said I owed him. I said it wasn't my fault. He had his chance. He was on the court, not me."

eight

Throughout the 1975–76 basketball season Walter Luckett played in a number of semiprofessional leagues such as the United States Basketball League and the Eastern Basketball League. He was paid about $50 per game but claimed to his friends he was paid $150 per game plus expenses. Most of those leagues played their games in high school gyms throughout the East, like the one in Roxbury, Massachusetts, which had a cork floor scarred with a thousand cigarette burns. In the middle of winter it was unheated. When Walt saw that gym he let out an involuntary gasp. "My God!" he said, "even I feel sorry for myself." He noted it was quite a comedown for someone who had played in the 14,000-seat Convocation Center at the University of Ohio. But no matter how depressing his surroundings, he vowed that he would continue in his quest to return to the NBA.

"When I first came home," he says, "I hated the world. I didn't leave my house for weeks. It was the first time in my life I didn't have a goal every day. I felt I belonged in P. T. for the rest of my life. Before that I had always wanted to stand out, to be different. Now I hated basketball. I never wanted to play again. Then I got some offers to play in various leagues and I started working out again. I realized this was no time for foolish pride, that there was no way that I wasn't a pro player. Yet, I wasn't there. Why not? It must be politics. I vowed to give it three more years because God had given me this gift and I wasn't using it."

Playing against teams that rarely rose to the caliber of competition he experienced in college, and whose players were often out of shape and talentless, Walter Luckett averaged about twenty points a game. He looked no better or worse than he had in college. In fact, many of his friends, like Don Clemmons, claimed that the Walter Luckett they had known in high school would have averaged forty points a game in these same leagues. "John Brisker was sitting on the bench in the NBA," says Clemmons "when he got sent down to the Eastern League. In each of his first two games he scored over fifty points, and he was back in the NBA a few days later. That's the kind of thing Walter had to show to get back there, but he didn't."

Walter played a timid game in the Eastern League. He would take only the safest jump shots from no more than fifteen feet away. And even then he would shoot only when forced to—that is, only when he found himself clear. He would take a few seconds to set the ball in his hands, as if shooting a foul shot, then take his jumper. He seldom looked to make his own shot, but settled instead for what was given him. In one game in Roxbury, his team was behind with a few seconds left to play when they devised a play to spring Walter free for a shot. He couldn't get free; someone else took the team's last shot and missed. After the game Clemmons claimed Walter did not try hard enough to get free. "He didn't really want to take it," said Clemmons. Walter claims his new reticence was merely a desire to play a conservative game. "I can't just heave 'em up," he says. He claimed that he was trying to play an ideal game in his head, even if the players he played with and against could not adjust to his vision of how that game should be played. Many of his friends felt, however, that Walter was just giving them an excuse for the fact he had grown timid over the years.

While Walter Luckett was playing in the Eastern League and Frank Oleynick was playing in the NBA, Barry McLeod was completing his final season at Centenary College. Over his first two years as a starter Barry had guided Centenary to 21–4 and 25–4 records, and now in his senior year he would guide the team to a 23–5 season. He would not, however, fulfill his ambition of leading them to a national championship because Centenary was put on probation by the NCAA in Barry's freshman year for alleged recruiting violations involving their seven-foot center, Robert Parish. This was one of Barry's most bitter disappointments in basketball. He had had to take a back seat in personal glory to Frank and Walter once in college, and he had always felt that the only way he could redeem himself in his own eyes, and theirs, was to lead his team to the kind of championship seasons neither Frank nor Walter could produce for their schools.

Barry's senior year was further clouded by the death of his mother from cancer. It was not a surprise to him —she had been suffering for many months—but still it hit him extremely hard. He remembers the last time he saw her. It was during the basketball season. "Things were happening so fast with her," he says, "that I had to leave the team and go home. I was trying to concentrate on playing ball because I knew I had a chance to be drafted by the pros, and I was worrying about my mother too. When I got home I just moped around the house for days. She was in bed all the time, but she knew what was going on in my mind. She said, 'What's the matter with you, boy? You in love or something?' Then she said, 'I know I'm gonna die soon, and so do you. You gotta pick yourself up, boy.' She was a very tough woman. Sometimes I think she was too hard on me. Other times, well, some of the things she told me I never forgot. Like the time Frank and I were going away to college for the first time and she said to me, 'Your cousin will be a professional basketball player someday, and maybe you will too. But even if you don't, you'll be a great coach.' I never forgot that."

Barry became the only one of the three friends to earn his college degree, in physical education. Since he was always thought least bright of the three, he is justifiably proud of that degree. Also, like his cousin and Walter Luckett, Barry was drafted by an NBA team when his college career was over, at the end of his senior year. In the spring of 1976 he was chosen in the seventh round by the Chicago Bulls.

For Frank Oleynick, the 1975–76 basketball season was the most frustrating of his career up until that time. It began auspiciously enough with his large bonus and attendant publicity, and continued on an encouraging note through his team's exhibition season. Frank played considerably during those preseason games, averaging close to fifteen points a game. At the time he was Seattle's third guard, behind Fred Brown and Slick Watts. Fred

Brown was a former ABA standout renowned for brilliant jump shooting; he was nicknamed "Downtown" Freddy Brown because of the distance from which he launched those jump shots. He was, however, vastly deficient in the other parts of the game—defense, ball handling, passing—and so of limited value to the Sonics. Watts, on the other hand, was a quick, deceptive player whose value lay in his ability to penetrate to the basket before feeding off to one of his teammates, and in stealing the opposition's passes. He was a poor shooter, however, and a limited player who could not start with many other NBA teams. He was a flamboyant character both on and off the court. With his shaved head, he looked like a small "Mr. Clean," and the Seattle fans loved him for this and his infectious enthusiasm. He was a great drawing card in Seattle, and it would be difficult for Bill Russell to replace him without hurting the team's attendance. But Russell planned to make that move anyway, and he told Frank before the season began that by season's end Frank would replace Watts in the starting lineup.

Russell's plan, to move Frank gradually into the Sonics' lineup that year, was changed drastically by two circumstances. Just before the season began the Sonics acquired veteran guard Herm Gilliam from the Atlanta Hawks. At the time Gilliam was out of shape, so Russell continued to favor Frank over him as the team's third guard. Secondly, at the beginning of the season the Sonics did not figure to make the NBA playoffs and so Russell could afford to move a rookie like Frank into the lineup. But once the schedule began and the Sonics showed signs of being able to earn a playoff berth, Russell decided to use the veteran Gilliam as a third guard instead of Frank. This did not alter Russell's opinion of Frank as one of the players he counted on in the future. It was just that the future was now a little more distant than it had been at the beginning of the season.

The change in status and playing time made Frank increasingly bitter. He took out his bitterness on Slick Watts, whom he saw as his rival. More than once during practice Frank would manhandle Watts in the hope that he could incite him to fight. But Watts could not be angered. Whenever Watts' name came up in a conversation, Frank would say contemptuously, "If Slick had hair he'd be playing in the Eastern League."

Bill Bradley, the former Knicks' player, wrote in his book, *Life on the Run*, that for an NBA rookie, playing time is like food—without it, he would starve. It was doubly important for a player of Frank's talent since he needed playing time to keep his skills tuned properly. Dave Bike, his assistant coach at Seattle U., once said that Frank needed more playing and practice time than most players because his skills were of a more delicate balance than those of most players. "Frank's game wasn't natural, it was learned," says Bike. "And so it could be forgotten if Frank didn't get a chance to use it every day. Also, the things he did required more practice because they were so refined, like dribbling behind his back. The more Frank practiced and played, the more easily things came to him. Whenever he didn't practice much he looked sloppy."

The 1975–76 season held only isolated instances of satisfaction for Frank Oleynick. They were brilliant flashes sustained only for brief moments, highly valued in the ghetto but only hinting at Frank's potential. In Madison Square Garden one night against the New

York Knicks, Frank Oleynick fakes Earl Monroe left, then drives along the baseline and dunks the ball through the basket to a chorus of "Frankie! Frankie!" from his black friends in the stands. When Frank entered that game late in the third period, his Sonics were behind by eight points, primarily due to Monroe's scoring. But when Frank left the game early in the fourth period after playing for eight minutes, his team was ahead thanks to Frank having shut out Monroe defensively during that period. In another game in Philadelphia against the 76ers, Frank leads a fast break and, confronted by Sixers' guard Doug Collins, pulls a spin move that leaves Collins gasping in pain on the floor with a sprained ankle. And in Boston Garden one night, Frank fakes the Celtics' Charley Scott so devastatingly that Scott dives into the stands while Frank takes a deliberate and uncontested jump shot. Swish! After that game, in a Boston hotel room, Sonny James appears, dressed in a short fitted leather jacket and patchwork jeans. His eyes are glassy as he tells Frank how he had confronted Charley Scott the night before in a Boston bar.

"Charley Scott's a night person," says Sonny. "He's got a nice game, I guess, but he don't excite me. Him and his Mercedes-Benz. I went up to him in this bar and said, 'Charley Scott, I got a home boy on the Sonics whose gonna get his shit off on you.' Charley Scott say, 'By the name of Oleynick?' I say, 'Yeh.' And he say, 'I heard of him.' I told Scott, Russ's got no business starting Slick ahead of you, and that's the truth." Sonny is referring to Bill Russell, whom he has never met but whom he speaks of as if an acquaintance or, at very least, an equal.

Sonny takes great pleasure in telling that Scott story because Frank Oleynick is his pride and joy. Frank is doing things in NBA games that he learned from watching Sonny James years ago on Pitt Street. Even Frank admits that Sonny was the most talented basketball player ever to come out of Bridgeport. If not for drugs and his bank robberies, he might be in Frank's place. Sonny thinks so too, which is why, when he was in Boston to watch Frank play that night, he called up Red Auerbach, the Celtics general manager, and asked him for a tryout. Without irony, Sonny says to Auerbach, "You know, your backcourt men, Havlicek, Scott and White, ain't gettin' any younger." When he relates this story to Frank in that Boston hotel room, there are no snickers from those assembled; only a nodding of heads of those who still believe in Sonny's magic. Even if Sonny had been given a tryout by Auerbach that day, it would not have done him much good. A few weeks later he was arrested for armed bank robbery, and today he is serving twenty years to life in prison.

Whenever Frank was given extended playing time by Russell, he responded more than adequately. One night in San Francisco he scored eighteen points against All-Star guard Phil Smith. Another night in New Orleans, against The Jazz, he scored twenty-two points and fed off to Fred Brown for fifteen more. Brown totaled forty points that night, and after the game Russell told Frank that the team's offense ran smoother than it had all year with him at the helm. Yet Frank did not play the next few games. Of Russell's thinking, Frank says, "I don't know what's going on in his mind. I have no idea."

Those games of extended playing time were few during the season. To keep his skills honed, Frank spent a lot of time in gyms, practicing alone or with whomever he could find. "I wasn't gettin' a helluva lot of playing time," he says, "so I'd go to the gym and play pickup games with any gym rats I could find. One day—I hadn't played in a week—I went to the basket like I had a million times before. I got my feet tangled up and hit my knee squarely on the floor. I couldn't run that night during our drills, so I gave up. They took an arthrogram, which showed I had torn ligaments. I was scared. I didn't know what the fuck to do. Russell talked to me and told me it would be best to get it operated on right away. They tied the ligaments together and I was put in a cast to my hip.

"After the operation, Russell told me he was just about to give me more playing time as we approached the playoffs. He admitted that he had made a mistake not giving me more playing time during the year. I told him I thought all along he was making a mistake. He said he should have played me ahead of Gilliam. He's not the kind of guy to bullshit you, you know. I know Russell's reputation for not liking whites, but I never thought his decision was a black-white thing. In my association with him, I have the utmost respect for him as a man. I kinda think he likes me a little bit. He was always talking to me. He helped when I was looking to buy a house in Seattle. It was on the water and would have cost me over $100,000. He told me to wait a bit. Then he said, 'You got fancy taste, don't you, boy?' Later when we made the playoffs and then were eliminated, Russell told me that he thought we could have won it if I had played at the end. In the last few games before I was hurt I had had twenty-point games against Phoenix and Kansas City."

Because he felt he would be unable to help the team during the playoffs, and because he was depressed over his injury and lonesome for his friends back in Bridgeport, Frank left Seattle and returned home. Although he would soon return to Seattle, it was a decision that would haunt him. Says Bruce Webster, a friend, "Whenever things get rough for Frank he's got to go back to the Terrace. He'll never really leave it."

"It all just came out," says Frank. "I got bad press for leaving the team. But I was in a cast to my hip and I was pretty hard to get along with. I did the hospital routine, then stayed alone at my apartment. I read books and made over $400 in telephone calls. Finally I decided this was ridiculous, so I went home. I couldn't see myself cheering the guys from the bench. I was bitter inside. Russell said it was all right to leave. Anyway, after the playoffs things came out in the papers where guys like Freddy Brown said I shoulda stayed with the club. They didn't like my leaving, so when it came time to vote on playoff shares, they only voted me half a share. I wasn't even notified about the meeting to vote. It was all pretty fucked up. They voted a black player—Abdul Assiz (Don Smith)—half a share and he only played in our last twenty games. They gave nothing to another white player, John Hummer, a Princeton graduate. He stormed into Russell's office and told him the vote was chicken shit. He said it showed no class and had racial overtones. Russell made the team take a second vote, and they took part of my money and gave it to Hummer. Now I get a one-third share and he gets a quarter share. The black players tried to make a joke of it, saying I had all that bonus money and my Mercedes and all, and that I didn't need it. But that wasn't the point. It wasn't big money, the difference between $4000 and $2000 for me, but I was upset. I let it pass, though.

"It had begun to dawn on me that things couldn't

be like they were back in Bridgeport. In Bridgeport I grew up in a friendly black atmosphere. I won their respect on my playing and my personality. But in the NBA everyone can play, and color is just too big a barrier. Even with my background. You never see whites and blacks together after the game. And yet, all my associations had always been with blacks, and now I couldn't hang with them. It's funny, me, who's totally different from all the whites on the team, was thrown back with whites for the first time in my life. And I had nothing in common with them. But I learned from that experience. It opened up another part of the world for me. Now I enjoy guys like Hummer, a real Ivy Leaguer but a great guy. He was my best friend on the team, and yet, if we were back in Bridgeport, I never would have hung with him."

This fact of reverse prejudice in the NBA was almost as difficult for Frank to adjust to as his lack of playing time. There were other difficult adjustments that first year. "NBA life is a bitch," he says. "The travel is tough. You play in a different city almost every night. The glory of playing in the NBA wore off me after our first thirteen-day road trip. And there are some ridiculous wild guys in the league. There's a lot of drug stuff. It surprised me. I'm a health nut and drugs are not conducive to health. Some guys I liked, I lost respect for when I saw how they took care of themselves. I've seen a lot of guys who didn't fulfill their potential. A lot of guys would be better people if they didn't play basketball. I think Walter Luckett would be a better person if he didn't play basketball. But that's kinda fucked up even for me to be saying because I owe everything I have to basketball. And at Seattle I never got caught up in the things the other guys did. I stayed mostly to myself. I was a loner. I led a low-key life in my apartment. I listened to music mostly. It was partly a black-and-white thing. There's a lot of prejudice in the NBA. The blacks are on top. My friendship with blacks had always been to my advantage, but it didn't do me any good with the Sonics."

When the season ended, Frank returned to Bridgeport for the summer. He had Russell's promise that if he got his leg in shape and was ready to play by the fall, he would receive plenty of playing time during the coming season. Frank approached that rehabilitation project with enthusiasm. He was determined to regain the form he had had at Seattle U. and to become a great NBA player. He was also enthusiastic about being reunited with his cousin, Barry McLeod. They had not seen each other much over the last three years, and now for the first time in that span they could pick up the relationship they had had all their lives. Barry was enthusiastic about the summer too, since he had been drafted by the Chicago Bulls and would report to their training camp in late summer. He and Frank would work each other into shape playing in all the gyms and on all the street corners as when they were younger. Even Walter Luckett had something to look forward to: The Detroit Pistons had promised him a second tryout in the late summer, and he was determined to make the best of this second chance. His attitude toward Frank had softened, and he was anxious to renew what had been their earlier friendship, although he admitted it would be on a different level. He would no longer be on top, as before. In fact, he now spoke of Frank helping him regain the form that had once made him the greatest high school basketball player in the country.

nine

9 A.M. Frank Oleynick, his elbow casually resting on the windowsill of his meticulously kept chocolate Mercedes-Benz, is driving on the Connecticut Thruway overlooking the city of Bridgeport. Smoke rises from the stacks of a dozen factories. It is a bright summer day. Sunlight streams in through the car's open sunroof. Music from his stereo tape deck surrounds him. "I appreciate my life-style now," he says. He looks incongruously baby-faced behind the wheel of this big car. He is wearing a T-shirt and sweat pants and unlaced sneakers. But, in a way, he looks so relaxed behind the wheel that he seems to belong there. "I've always liked fine things," he continues. "Ever since I was a kid. Some people like them but don't appreciate them. I do. I take care of my ride. I keep it clean. I take care of my crib too. And my music. It keeps me up. I love music. Elton John is the joint, even if he is a white boy. And Scott Herron, he's the greatest, you know—"Home is where the hatred is." That's the truth. I don't let nobody fuck with my music, my ride or my crib. And my game. Nobody fucks with my game."

Frank is on his way to pick up his cousin, Barry McLeod, and then Walter Luckett, with whom he is going to have lunch today. It is the end of summer and all three friends have long since renewed the relationships they had years ago. There is only one difference: Today Frank is on top. The others are his satellites, and he takes great pleasure in this ironic turn of events.

"Walt's got a lot of problems now," he continues. "It hasn't been gravy for him lately. That *Sports Illustrated* piece was the worst thing that could have happened to him. He felt he had already earned it without playing one game of college ball. Now he's gotta get a decent outlook. I mean, last year he went to Detroit and he tells me Archie Clark stinks. He's gonna burn this guy and that guy. I tell him those guys are in the NBA, man, they're gonna burn his shit. I know those guys. Just the other day he started that shit—we were over Barry's shooting hoops outside—so I told him off. He gets embarrassed and comes over and points a finger in my face and says, 'You know what your problem is, boy? You get hot. You don't listen. I don't get emotional like you.' I just laughed at him, and he left. Walter's too sensitive. You always got to worry about what you say with him, man, worry about his feelings. Well, I stopped worrying about his feelings when I was fifteen years old. That's for children, not men.

"But I think Walt's gonna make it this year with Detroit. His game is better than people think. You just watch us play together today. Walter plays better when he's with me and Barry. We inspire him. He gets his confidence just being on the court with us. He's a very unselfish player. He never shot enough, not even in high school. He was a fantastic shooter, but poor defensively. But now that he's lost some of his shooting he's got to compensate by playing other parts of the game. I think he can do it. He just has to have in his mind that he's not Walter Luckett anymore when he goes out to Detroit. I'll be very surprised if he doesn't make it. Maybe I'm prejudiced. I feel partly responsible for what happened to his career. I like Walter. I don't want to hurt him. Shit, I almost love Walter Luckett."

Frank guides the big Mercedes down Chamberlain Avenue, a narrow street of tiny closely situated Cape Cod homes. It is a well-kept neighborhood, half-white, half-black. He stops in front of Barry's house and beeps the horn. It is a house like all the others, except there is a basket on a pole in the driveway. While he waits for Barry, Frank says, "Oh, Barry's an asshole. He's out drinking beer all night, then he don't want to get up until noon. He's just starting to open his eyes at 3 P.M. About midnight, he comes alive." He laughs to himself, then adds, "I been trying to teach Barry that when he makes Chicago he shouldn't buy a Cadillac, like Walter. That's a bad investment. You lose $5000 when you drive it out of the showroom. A Mercedes is an investment. But I can't tell him nothing 'cause I'm higher up now. It's the same with Walter. It's too bad for them, because you gotta be humble to be good. When we were kids Barry was my protector. Now, it's different. But still he's pretty serious, really. His mother's death hit him pretty hard. He feels all he's got left is to make Chicago. I hope he does, but it's gonna be tough. Centenary hurt Barry because he only did certain things there. It stifled his game. He used to bring the ball up real slow—he played the point—and monopolize it. He doesn't move without the ball, he's used to always having it. I told him in the pros you got to give it up. But he won't listen. Stupid! Shit, I know more about the game than him and Walter put together. I may love Barry McLeod, but I'm still the best."

Barry finally emerges from the house, in a state of half-undress. He has no shirt on. He is wearing sweat pants and low-cut sneaks that are unlaced. The heels of his feet crush the heels of his sneaks. It is a habit of dress he picked up from blacks in Louisiana. Frank calls it the affectation of "a country boy." Barry is a tough-looking youth with a close-cropped, Roman haircut. He gets into the car and says nothing. Frank says, "Hello, asshole." Barry grunts. He is half asleep. Frank laughs out loud—"See, I told ya"—as he backs the car out of the driveway.

10 A.M. Frank and Barry move through Bridgeport's Main Street, past deserted storefronts and an occasional new building, in search of Walter's aqua-blue Cadillac. As they move downtown people notice them, stop, smile and wave. The people are mostly black, young and old. Barry and Frank comment on the wavers as they wave back, usually in the form of a black power, clenched-fist salute. Their comments range from junkie, to basketball, to doing time in the joint. Those people are waving, they say, because the sight of Frank's car is a reminder to them that one of their own has made it.

Finally awake, Barry says, "Where we gonna meet Stupid?"

Frank says, "I don't know. He said he'll be someplace downtown."

Barry shakes his head in disgust. He does not like the idea that Walter did not give him and Frank a prearranged meeting place. Both he and Frank complain that blacks do not appreciate time. They don't value appointments. Then Barry says, "Walter can be a grind, you know. He's too sensitive. You got to watch what you say.

And he don't trust anyone anymore. He thinks everyone is out to get him. You see, the thing is, Walter Luckett is not a happy man. He's torn. There's a turmoil in his mind. Like the other day, we played together in this tournament in Stamford. Cedric Cannon, he plays for Iona College, he asked me to play with them. I say, 'What about Luckett?' He say, 'Ah!' I say, 'Well, you got to get in touch with him outta respect. He's a Bridgeport boy.' Cedric said he'd leave it up to me. Well, the first night we played, everyone was relaxed. Walter got twenty points, I got seventeen and we had a good sweat. I just wanted to have some fun, man, be free, know what I mean? Then Walter heard they were gonna have an MVP trophy and one for the highest scorer. The next night he just dogged us out. He shot his ass off. He had to be the big deal. He demanded that he play guard. I tell him he's the biggest man on the court and to go under the basket. He say, 'Playing forward ain't gonna help me with Detroit.' He was walking around with his hands on his hips, copping an attitude. We almost got into it. I wouldn't talk to him all the way home. Maybe it was just the crowd, people watching him.

"When we play pickup games with no one around, he don't act like that. When he plays with me and Frank, he's happy again. He's with friends. The other day we played on the same team in a pickup game and Frank and I got the ball to Walter and then we cleared out. 'Go ahead,' we said. 'Take 'em, Walter.' He knew by our expressions that we had confidence in him. He went into his thing like he can do and he got on top of the situation. But that only happens sometimes. Other times he just stands around. He's easy to check. He don't move to get the ball. He's used to everyone working hard to get him the ball. His game don't have much variety. In high school he was so much bigger than everyone else, all he had to do was take that J. He never had to work on anything else. Nobody could stop his J. Now he stands in the corner and claps for the ball. Walt checks himself, see. He lets guys who shouldn't even be on the same court with him check him. Watching him now, I don't think he's as good as I always thought he was. Maybe he never was.

"Sometimes, too, I wonder if Walter loves the game. Maybe he's just trying to make the NBA because that's what he's been programmed for all his life. I don't think he's as smart as I once thought. But don't get me wrong. Walter Luckett can play the game, man. I don't want to get into what's in his head, but he can play the game. If he don't make it, it's not 'cause he don't have it. Maybe he just don't have the killer instinct anymore. He used to have it. I feel Frank learned that from him. In Frank's embryonic stage. . . ."

"Oh, what the fuck you talkin' about . . . embryonic stage," says Frank, and he laughs with mock disgust. But Barry is serious.

"In Frank's infant stage he learned from Walter Luckett. We all did. We had his guidance ahead of us, to learn from and shoot for. He helped us all, not as a person but as a symbol. That's why I want him to make it so badly. He was the best before all of us were anything. He came with respects when my mother died."

Finally Frank spots Walter's car. Walter is standing alongside it, searching in his pockets for a dime to drop in the parking meter. Frank pulls up and gets out to talk.

In the car, Barry says, "I get along better with

Walt than Frank does. Frank and Walter will always be rivals. I keep telling Frank I'm gonna buy a Cadillac like Walter just to piss him off. It used to be Frank and me never disagreed on anything. But now I sense we're spreading out. If we weren't cousins and so close, there might have been trouble between us at times. We both got these big egos. I mean, I think when I get on the court I'm better than Frank Oleynick and Walter Luckett both. But Frank's the only one who made it. Why? He's been lucky. I mean, what if he hurt his leg before he signed? See what I mean? Frank's lucky. Lucky! Lucky! Lucky! I slept in the same bed with him. Man, he ain't my cousin, he's my blood. I love Frank Oleynick. But why him? Why not me? He got it and I don't. Luck! Luck! I'm the baddest in this city, man."

11 A.M. Frank Oleynick, Walter Luckett and Barry McLeod are sitting in Frank's car outside of a hot dog stand near Beardsley Park in Bridgeport. They are in various states of sprawl, talking, kidding one another as they eat.

"You played like an asshole yesterday," says Frank to Walter.

"That's why you lost," says Walter.

"I lost 'cause I played like I should, but the assholes I was playing with played like you."

"Uh-huh, uh-huh," nods Walter in mock agreement. Then, worried, he says, "You think they gonna tow my car, Frankie? I didn't put no dime in the meter."

"Whatcha worryin' about?" says Frank. "If you got the money for that big Cadillac, you got money to pay a fine. Besides, you got friends in city hall, don't you? I mean, you're Walter Luckett, ain't you?" Walter does not laugh at this. He is truly worried about having his car towed away. Frank jabs him again. "If you wasn't so cheap, Luckett, maybe you woulda put a dime in the meter."

"Fuck you!" says Walter. Just then a pretty black girl gets out of a car and goes to the hot dog stand. Walter, Frank and Barry stare after her.

"That's bad, man," says Frank.

"What's this shit, *Mandingo* all over again?" says Walter, laughing. "White masters and their black slaves! Ha! At night Frankie be going to the Terrace for you know what. While he be in the Terrace, I be in Fairfield, man, the suburbs. White folk, you know. You forget who educated your ass, Frankie. I hooked you up with black chicks."

"Oh, blow it outta your ass, Walter Luckett," says Frank. "You never educated me to nothing."

"Oh, Frankie," laughs Walter. "You was awful shy in high school. Then you broke out in your senior year. You made All-State in basketball and then you thought you was All-State with the ladies. Ha, ha, ha!"

"Bullshit! Bullshit!" says Frank. "Yesterday you stunk, Walter Luckett. You shit on ice. I wouldn't let you play that way if you was on my team."

"That's why me and Barry hook up," says Walter. "Me and Barry are bitches together."

"Yeh, I think you two doing each other."

"Barry pitches the ball out to me and I fire that J." Walter turns to Barry, who has yet to come to life, and lays out his palms. Barry slaps five.

"That J ain't making you a better player," says Frank. "If I play with you I make you work."

"Your problem is you pout instead of hustling back

on defense, boy," says Walter. "Attitude! Attitude! Attitude! Sharpen it up, boy!"

"Blow it outta your ass, Luckett. I hope your motherfucking car is gone when we get back. I think I'll let you walk back to your house. You got money for cab fare, don't you, boy? The walk will be good for you. You're lazy. You just like Barry. I go by his house and he still sleeping. Shit, next time I ain't gonna wait on him."

"Patience, brother, patience. That's your problem."

"If he don't respect me I ain't gonna respect him."

"Barry McLeod! Barry McLeod! He is the best," says Walter.

Barry, coming to life, says, "Walter Luckett! Walter Luckett! The best ever to come out of the state."

Frank makes a disgusted motion with his head toward his two friends. "Now, I know you two doing each other. Heckle and Jeckle. Ha!"

Walter, turning to Barry, says, "Frank say he not gonna cater to you no more. He say he not your hotel service wake-up."

"Fuck him," says Barry.

"Fuck you both," says Frank. "You both washouts. You okay in my book, Walter. For an hour a day. Then I can't stand you."

"A good human being, I am," says Walter.

"You an asshole, brother. You shoot from so far out you gonna get a hernia someday."

"Barry! Barry! Barry! Reinforcement!"

"Hello, brother," says Barry. "You are the greatest." Walter grins.

After they finish their hot dogs they drive back to Walter's car. It is still there. Walter smiles. Then the three friends make plans to meet later at the Fairfield University gym for a workout. Fairfield University, unlike the University of Bridgeport, is a suburban white school whose students and basketball players are predominantly white. Their coach, Fred Barakat, is an opportunistic man who always seems to make the best of a situation. For instance, he got Walter Luckett to speak at one of his summer basketball clinics for nothing. Frank refused to do the same. Before Walter gets out of the car, Frank chides him for being so gullible.

"You got nothing for speaking, you fool."

"I did, huh? Well, I got the use of the gym for us today. What goes around, comes around."

"You coulda got it anyway," says Frank. "You helping Barakat just by being in that gym, man. You draw people. You're Walter Luckett." Frank is not kidding now. "I did it last year [spoke at Barakat's clinic] and it ain't shit. White boys who can't play but their family's got money. All you are is a baby-sitter. I rather go to U.B. or the Terrace and rap. I'm not gonna be no fucking baby-sitter for a buncha white boys."

"You got a bad attitude, boy," says Walter as he gets out of the car, shaking his head seriously.

"I'll have my own camp someday," Frank yells after him. "And I'll have the best players work at it. I'll have you at my camp, Walter Luckett."

As Walter walks over to his car, Barry says, "Barakat butters up Walter and the fucker falls for it." He shakes his head. Walter is about to get into his car when he notices something attached to his windshield wiper. He takes it off and stares at it. It is an orange parking ticket. He puts both hands on his hips in disgust and looks over at Frank and Barry. They begin to laugh as they pull away. Frank calls out to Walter, "Send it to Barakat!"

Noon. Frank and Barry are driving through the Terrace looking for Don Clemmons, with whom they are going to the beach for a while before they meet Walter Luckett at Fairfield U. As always, no matter where Frank goes in his car, blacks stop and wave to him. In fact, they are so in love with Frank and Barry and, to a much lesser extent, with Walter, that a few nights ago the entire Terrace community gave all three a going-away party in preparation for their leaving for their respective NBA summer camps. It is ironic that Frank accepted that day for him, because when his own father wanted to organize such a testimonial, Frank told him the time wasn't right for it. His father did not understand and was hurt. But Frank was nonetheless thrilled with the day the blacks in the Terrace had given the three of them.

"It was the best time ever," says Frank.

"The best time ever," echoes Barry. "Even Walter said so."

"Sumpter organized it," says Barry. "He got a lot of guys to put up ten dollars. Me and Frank did, too. Walter didn't want to put up his money unless he was guaranteed he'd get it back. At the end of the party Walter goes up to Harrison Taylor and asks for his money. Harrison says to him, 'I put up $100 for your party and I didn't get nothing back, and you want your money? Get the fuck outta here!'"

"But it was a wild time," says Frank. "The whole Terrace social hall was filled. Everyone was black except me and Barry. The women had made chicken and potato salad and there was dancing all night long. Sweat, man, everybody was sweating and drinking and laughing. I left early, about 2:30 A.M. Barry, he got fucked up. He stayed until 5 A.M."

"Yeh," says Barry. "It was wild. They even had these two bodyguards at the door to make sure everyone came up with a dollar to get in. Man, one of them had strong features, know what I mean? You can see everything, his stuff all hangs out. He's the toughest guy in Bridgeport. His partner was a boxer. They both been in the joint, I think. Man, nobody messes with them. One guy who come up to the door was, oh, about 6-3, 250 pounds, and when they asked for a dollar he say, 'A dollar!' They put a knife to his throat and pushed him up against the wall. They picked him up by the legs and was gonna throw him down the stairs if he didn't come up with his dollar." Barry laughs to himself. "Yes, sir, I guess you could say them boys took an excess of enthusiasm to their jobs. Beyond the call of duty, you might say."

"I love the Terrace," says Frank. "If I was playing for the Knicks I'd still be here."

Frank stops his car in front of a small Cape Cod house on the outskirts of the Terrace. He blows his horn and waits. After a few minutes he blows it again and curses Don Clemmons, who, he says, is always late. Finally Clemmons comes out the door. He is a muscular black with a completely shaved head and one gold earring. But his fierce demeanor belies a gentle nature. He is carrying his one-year-old son, a carrot-topped baby with huge light eyes, naked except for a diaper. Clemmons gets into the car and immediately Frank takes his son and puts him on his lap. The baby's eyes grow even larger as Frank lets him steer the car down Cedar Street and out of the Terrace. They are heading for a private beach in Fairfield.

"Heh, boy, watch the road," says Frank. Then he adds, "Well, say goodbye to Cedar Street, boy. Today, you're going to Rainbow Road and the good life."

1 P.M. When word gets around Bridgeport that Frank, Barry and Walter will be having a run at the Fairfield U. gym, dozens of the best basketball players in the city, most of them black, appear at the gym at the precise time Frank and Barry arrive. Walter has not yet showed up. Among the players are Cedric Cannon, a starter at Iona College as a freshman; Phil Ness, Lafayette College's center and leading scorer; Don Clemmons, a former junior college top scorer; Phil Nastu, the high scorer on the University of Bridgeport team; and Ron DelBianco, the childhood friend of Frank and Barry's. The most talented of all the players, however, is a junior in high school named Wes Matthews, who in his senior year will be named to most first-team high school All-American teams. He is a cocky black who more than holds his own with the older players on the court. Another of the players to appear at Fairfield U. is Len Morales, a chunky, handsome youth of twenty-four with large, sad chocolate eyes. He was once a great college prospect in high school and is regarded by his peers as the best Puerto Rican basketball player ever to come out of the city. But then, in high school, he got involved in what his peers call "the street scene." By the time he moved away from it he was too old to forge either a collegiate or a professional career.

The game begins quickly after the players choose up sides. It is played full-court, without referees. It begins in orderly fashion with each team setting up plays and trying to make precise passes, but after awhile, when the players tire, it degenerates into a racehorse city game of fastbreaking while weary players trail the field. Walter Luckett does not arrive until most of the players are exhausted. Frank claims that Walter's late arrival is a sign of an ego problem. He must show his "cool" by arriving late rather than early. To appear early would be a sign of enthusiasm not considered "cool" in certain black circles. Walter is immediately given to Frank's team and the game continues, nonstop, for another half hour. During that time, Frank and Walter work beautifully together. Whenever Walt gets a rebound he pitches it out to Frank and then streaks up court, to be fed again by Frank for an easy fastbreak basket. Frank has said, without envy, that if Walter played for the Seattle Supersonics, Frank would feed him the ball and make him a star. He does so today for about thirty minutes and then, exhausted, he and Barry quit the game. As soon as they quit everyone else does. Walter is upset. He has only played for thirty minutes and barely worked up a sweat. Outside in the parking lot Walter pulls his car alongside Frank's and shouts, "When I come you all quit and don't want to run."

"You came a fucking hour late," says Frank. "We're running our ass off in the hot gym and you ain't even here.... Go put your long face back in your car."

"I wanted to run and you take your shoes off like you was King Kong. You motherfucker, you look like him, and you smell like him, too."

"Why you long-faced sonuvabitch! Come here, you Dick Van Dyke-faced motherfucker."

"You look like Casper the Friendly Ghost."

"Blow it outta your ass, Fang."

"Walter, we're bringing you to Newtown tonight," says Barry, referring to the site of the state mental institution.

"Walt, you are a sick fuck," says Frank. "You got teeth like piano keys."

"Go back to Lake Mohegan and take a swim," says Walt.

Don Clemmons comes over to the car and, looking first at Walter and then at Frank and Barry, says, "What's the problem? Luck got an attitude?"

"Yeh, he's a sick bastard," says Frank.

"Even your own boy, Blunt, disowned you," says Barry to Walter. "You're nothing but a long, foot-faced s.o.b. You a Converse face."

"Gimme your sneak," says Frank to Barry. "Quick, give it here!" Frank holds the shoe out the window, the sole facing Walter. "Here's your face, Luckett. You a foot-face." Walter waves his hand disgustedly at them and drives off. Frank yells after him, "Don't you run away from us, Converse face!" But he is gone. Finally Frank says to no one in particular, "Walt thinks we quit because he came. What the fuck? Fuck him. You know, you can't stay on the good side of that bastard for more than a day before he cops an attitude." Frank turns to Barry and says, "When Walter takes those forty-foot J's of his you shouldn't pass him the ball."

"I don't," says Barry.

"But he don't know why," says Frank. "He thinks it's because he's looking too good and you trying to keep him down. Oh, fuck him."

As they are about to leave, Frank notices Wes Matthews walking toward a car. He calls him over to his car.

"Why you avoiding me, boy?" says Frank.

"I ain't avoiding you," says Matthews, a proud, almost arrogant youth of seventeen.

"The hell you ain't. I gotta talk to you before I go, boy."

"I ain't goin' nowhere," says Matthews.

"Some other time, you hear?"

Later in the car, talking about Matthews' game, Barry wonders if he can shoot well enough to make it in big-team college basketball. Frank thinks so, but he is more worried about the youth's too cocky attitude than he is his shooting ability. That doesn't worry him, says Barry. "You know how them youngbloods are."

4 P.M. Frank's car is parked in front of Fernandez's grocery store in the east end of the city, a black and Puerto Rican section. Fernandez's is known for having the coldest bottles of beer in town. Ice is frozen to the bottles. Frank and a group of about ten friends, all black except for Barry and Len Morales, are sprawling about on the curb, drinking beer and talking.

"This is some ride, man," says Kenny Smalls, a tall, skinny black youth who started last year for North Carolina A & T when they played in Madison Square Garden. Smalls is sitting in the driver's seat of Frank's car, touching all the gadgets—sunroof, stereo tape deck, etc.—while drinking a bottle of Colt 45 Malt Liquor.

"Yeh, it's a nice ride," says Frank. Then, "You know, Kenny, I like your game. But you got to learn to give the ball up quicker, know what I mean? Don't worry, I'll get it back to you."

"Yeh, that's Wes Matthews' problem," says Len Morales, sitting on the curb, also drinking Colt 45. "But you can't talk to the boy. He got an attitude on him."

"I tried to tell him, too," says Willie Murphy, a tall, ascetic-looking black with a sharp goatee. "I told him to get rid of the ball, to throw it out without dribbling it all around, but he don't listen."

"He's just a youngblood, that's all," says Barry, leaning against Frank's car. "He almost got into it with Walter because Walter was climbing his back today. I told the boy not to take that shit from Walter."

"Yeh, but every time he drives to the basket," says Morales, "he thinks he's not supposed to get hit. He got to be able to take it."

"Somebody ought to talk to him," says Barry. "I think Frank will before he goes."

"I think you oughtta, too," says Morales. "And Walter Luckett."

"And you too," says Barry, and Morales lowers his head, as if embarrassed to be grouped in such company.

"But, still, I really like the boy's game," adds Barry. "He penetrates and feeds off. No Harding kid ever did that. They just ran and jumped because that's all their coach knew. Wes Matthews got it like me and Frank did, by watching television. By listening to Bill Russell talk, man. By memorizing the way those guys did it."

Inside the car Frank is showing Smalls pictures of his girl friend in Seattle, and her family's estate. Smalls looks at her house, shakes his head and says, without envy, "Man, that's some crib. Smokin'."

After about an hour there are dozens of empty Colt 45 bottles lined up on the curb running halfway down the block. After each youth finishes his beer he makes a point of placing the empty bottle neatly behind the others. The point is to make the line of bottles run to the end of the block. As the line lengthens, the youths grow more exuberant, less serious, and their talk turns inevitably back to their high school days, which for many of them were the high point of their lives. Cedric Cannon takes off his straw sombrero and makes a sweeping gesture to encompass the whole area around him. "This is my turf," he says. "It's the jointske. The land of the blue and gold [the colors of Harding High School]. I wish I could get back there, man. Some days."

"Who made you the mayor of this territory, boy?" says Frank. Then, as an afterthought, "Heh, where's Luckett? I thought he was supposed to come down here."

"He didn't come," says Barry, " 'cause he heard Sammy Miller gonna be here." Everyone laughs at this remark, refering to the half brother of Calvin Murphy, the NBA star. "Luckett don't dig Sammy 'cause Sammy steal his game. Sammy make Luckett cry." The others laugh at this, and as they do, a tall black man in tight cream-colored slacks appears. He is wearing clog-heeled shoes and a floral shirt tied above his waist to expose his navel. He is also wearing dark sunglasses and a high hairdo, somewhat like Little Richard's, the rock-and-roll star. His name is Larry Roberson. He is twenty-eight years old and was once a great basketball player at Central High School, where he refused to play basketball games on Friday night because he was then a practicing Seventh-Day Adventist. When reminded of his youthful religious zeal, Roberson says softly, with a smile, "Well, man, you know we all into different trips at different times."

"What you doin' now?" asks Barry.

"I'm into making little things," says Roberson. "I promote dances. A promoter, you might say."

"You still playing?" asks Barry.

Roberson shakes his head languidly. "Man, I'm too old. I'm an old dude, almost twenty-eight. I play a little tennis. But I don't chase it no more, know what I mean? New Haven. The Terrace. P.T. South Norwalk. Stamford. No siree, I don't chase the game no more."

epilogue

Walter Luckett lasted two weeks at the Detroit Pistons' fall training camp before he was released for the second time in his professional career. He left his Cadillac in Detroit and flew down to Atlanta to try out with the Hawks. When he was cut there, he took a bus back to Detroit to pick up his car. The bus trip took twenty-four hours. When Frank Oleynick heard about it he was angry. "Walt should have more pride than that," he says. "Pay the extra goddamned money and take a plane back! Time is worth more than money. Man, he's Walter Luckett, he ain't supposed to be riding no buses for twenty-four hours."

Barry McLeod lasted only two weeks at the Chicago Bulls' fall training camp before he was released also. He claims the Bulls had no intention of keeping him and that he never even had a chance to show his stuff. When he returned to Bridgeport he was so depressed he vowed never again to "chase the game." He went out nightly to the Terrace and drank vast quantities of beer until the early hours of the morning. Finally he began to vomit blood. One day he was rushed to the hospital seriously ill. A doctor told him he couldn't drink beer like he had been anymore without it being fatal—the same diagnosis

Barry's father had received years ago. Barry recuperated at his home on Chamberlain Avenue. As was his custom, he woke late in the afternoon and sat for hours in front of the television, like his father, and watched soap operas.

Frank Oleynick played the entire 1976–77 season with the Seattle Supersonics, a season even more frustrating than the last. Frank's knee had not quite healed properly and his lateral movement was severely limited. As a result, Bill Russell seldom used him. Frank took to sulking on the bench, fighting first privately then publicly with Russell, a man he once characterized as "the greatest human being I've ever met."

When asked about his relationship with Bill Russell, Frank would say, "There's no communication between us. I won't talk to him. I realize now that when he talked to me before, always telling me he's gonna play me on the next road trip, that it was just his way of discharging his obligation to me. He feels he did right by talking to me and so he can forget about playing me. The s.o.b. been lying to me all along. Who knows what's in his head? He does things nobody else would do just so people will think that Bill Russell knows things nobody else knows. Like he tells me that my playing time is dictated by the matchups of the team we're gonna play. Shit, if I don't play for five games, what does that tell me? It tells me I shouldn't fucking be in the NBA, that's what!" Finally, Frank fed the Seattle newspaper a story in which he blamed the Sonics' playing problems on Russell, and then demanded to be traded. No team in the league was interested in him, even though he had yet to turn twenty-two. In fact, when Kevin Loughery, the New York Nets' coach, was interviewed about a possible trade with Seattle, he said he was interested in anyone the Sonics had to offer except Oleynick.

Now when Frank entered hopelessly lost Seattle games he was out of shape and belligerently careless, no longer having that precarious fine tune he had so carefully cultivated before. He took long jump shots, almost defiantly, which often missed the basket completely. The Seattle fans, who had once loved him, now booed whenever he entered a game. Privately, Frank admitted that he could not bear to finish the season. He longed only to return to the Port and his friends.

"I thought Frank was grown up," says Barry. "But I guess he's only grown up in certain ways. I mean, man, he's in the NBA! He don't know how lucky he is! Sometimes he acts like a kid. He don't even try to make lay-ups during practice! They say Bill Russell hates to answer the telephone at night because he's afraid it's gonna be another problem with Frank. Shit, Frank's always jumping the club and coming back to the Port. It cost him $400 in fines. I told him to give me the money instead of Russell, I'll fly out to see him, he don't have to come home. But it's not a good sign. He's always crying to me. He say his knee is all right, but I hear Phil Smith scored eighteen points off him in a quarter this year. In college Frank shut him out. . . . I was gonna say something to Frank, but it's not my place."

Frank Oleynick was not released by the Seattle Supersonics until the late summer of 1977. He lasted only a few weeks in his third pro training camp before being let go by the Sonics' new coach, Bob Hopkins, a brother-in-law of Bill Russell. No other team in the NBA picked up Frank's option, since it would necessitate committing themselves to pay his high salary ($100,000) for the next three years. However, after Frank was officially waived out of the league, the Milwaukee Bucks offered him a tryout at the league minimum wage. Frank lasted a few weeks with the Bucks before he was cut. Then Indiana expressed interest in him and he flew there, only to be cut for the third time before the 1977 season had begun.

Frank returned to Seattle, cleaned out his apartment and prepared to fly back to Bridgeport. He sold his Mercedes-Benz, because by this time, after having supported his parents and bought them a house and a car, he was virtually broke. Soon after Frank returned home, his parents sold their house and moved into an apartment near Beardsley Park. He had gone through over $200,000 in two years. It was the first money he had ever earned.

During the winter of 1977–78, Frank Oleynick played with Walter Luckett in the Eastern Basketball League. They were teammates, for the first time in their lives, on the Quincy, Massachusetts, Chiefs. They each received $50 per game. Barry McLeod no longer plays the game.